STEPHEN KING

★ ★ ★ ★ ★ ★ ★ ★ ★ ★ ★ ★ ★ ★

STEPHEN KING

★ ★

AMY KEYISHIAN and MARJORIE KEYISHIAN

CHELSEA HOUSE PUBLISHERS

New York ★ Philadelphia

CHELSEA HOUSE PUBLISHERS

EDITORIAL DIRECTOR Richard Rennert
EXECUTIVE MANAGING EDITOR Karyn Gullen Browne
COPY CHIEF Robin James
PICTURE EDITOR Adrian G. Allen
CREATIVE DIRECTOR Robert Mitchell
ART DIRECTOR Joan Ferrigno
PRODUCTION MANAGER Sallye Scott

Pop Culture Legends
SENIOR EDITOR Kathy Kuhtz Campbell
SERIES DESIGN Basia Niemczyc

Staff for STEPHEN KING
ASSISTANT EDITOR Joy Sanchez
EDITORIAL ASSISTANT Scott D. Briggs
PICTURE RESEARCHER Sandy Jones
COVER ILLUSTRATION Steve Cieslawski

5 7 9 8 6 4

Library of Congress Cataloging-in-Publication Data

Keyishian, Amy.
Stephen King/Amy and Marjorie Keyishian.
p. cm.—(Pop culture legends)
Includes bibliographical references and index.
ISBN 0-7910-2340-0
     0-7910-2365-6 (pbk.)
1. King, Stephen, 1947—Biography—Juvenile literature. 2. Nov-
elists, American—20th century— Biography—Juvenile literature.
3. Horror tales—Authorship—Juvenile literature. [1. King,
Stephen, 1947– . 2. Authors, American.] I. Keyishian, Marjorie.
II. Series. III. Series.
PS3561.I483Z735 1995   94-37510
813'.54—dc20   CIP
[B]   AC

FRONTISPIECE:
Horror novelist Stephen King stands in front of his
Victorian mansion in Bangor, Maine. The immense
house is surrounded by a black wrought-iron fence,
complete with designs of bats and spiderwebs.

Contents ★ ★ ★ ★ ★ ★ ★ ★ ★ ★ ★ ★ ★ ★ ★ ★ ★ ★

A Reflection of Ourselves

Leeza Gibbons

I ENJOY A RARE PERSPECTIVE on the entertainment industry. From my window on popular culture, I can see all that sizzles and excites. I have interviewed legends who have left us, such as Bette Davis and Sammy Davis, Jr., and have brushed shoulders with the names who have caused a commotion with their sheer outrageousness, like Boy George and Madonna. Whether it's by nature or by design, pop icons generate interest, and I think they are a mirror of who we are at any given time.

Who are *your* heroes and heroines, the people you most admire? Outside of your own family and friends, to whom do you look for inspiration and guidance, as examples of the type of person you would like to be as an adult? How do we decide who will be the most popular and influential members of our society?

You may be surprised by your answers. According to recent polls, you will probably respond much differently than your parents or grandparents did to the same questions at the same age. Increasingly, world leaders such as Winston Churchill, John F. Kennedy, Franklin D. Roosevelt, and evangelist Billy Graham have been replaced by entertainers, athletes, and popular artists as the individuals whom young people most respect and admire. In surveys taken during each of the past 15 years, for example, General Norman Schwarzkopf was the only world leader chosen as the number-one hero among high school students. Other names on the elite list joined by General Schwarzkopf included Paula Abdul, Michael Jackson, Michael Jordan, Eddie Murphy, Burt Reynolds, and Sylvester Stallone.

More than 30 years have passed since Canadian sociologist Marshall McLuhan first taught us the huge impact that the electronic media have had on how we think, learn, and understand—as well as how we choose our heroes. In the 1960s, Pop artist Andy Warhol predicted that there would soon come a time when every American would be famous for 15 minutes. But if it is easier today to achieve Warhol's 15 minutes of fame, it is also much harder to hold on to it. Reputations are often ruined as quickly as they are made.

And yet, there remain those artists and performers who continue to inspire and instruct us in spite of changes in world events, media technology, or popular tastes. Even in a society as fickle and fast moving as our own, there are still those performers whose work and reputation endure, pop culture legends who inspire an almost religious devotion from their fans.

Why do the works and personalities of some artists continue to fascinate us while others are so quickly forgotten? What, if any, qualities do they share that enable them to have such power over our lives? There are no easy answers to these questions. The artists and entertainers profiled in this series often have little more in common than the enormous influence that each of them has had on our lives.

Some offer us an escape. Artists such as actress Marilyn Monroe, comedian Groucho Marx, and writer Stephen King have used glamour, humor, or fantasy to help us escape from our everyday lives. Others present us with images that are all too recognizable. The uncompromising realism of actor and director Charlie Chaplin and folk singer Bob Dylan challenges us to confront and change the things in our world that most disturb us.

Some offer us friendly, reassuring experiences. The work of animator Walt Disney and late-night talk show host Johnny Carson, for example, provides us with a sense of security and continuity in a changing world. Others shake us up. The best work of composer John Lennon and actor James Dean will always inspire their fans to question and reevaluate the world in which they live.

It is also hard to predict the kind of life that a pop culture legend will lead, or how he or she will react to fame. Popular singers Michael Jackson

and Prince carefully guard their personal lives from public view. Other performers, such as popular singer Madonna, enjoy putting their private lives before the public eye.

What these artists and entertainers do share, however, is the rare ability to capture and hold the public's imagination in a world dominated by mass media and disposable celebrity. In spite of their differences, each of them has somehow managed to achieve legendary status in a popular culture that values novelty and change.

The books in this series examine the lives and careers of these and other pop culture legends, and the society that places such great value on their work. Each book considers the extraordinary talent, the stubborn commitment, and the great personal sacrifice required to create work of enduring quality and influence in today's world.

As you read these books, ask yourself the following questions: How are the careers of these individuals shaped by their society? What role do they play in shaping the world? And what is it that so captivates us about their lives, their work, or the images they present?

Hopefully, by studying the lives and achievements of these pop culture legends, we will learn more about ourselves.

1 Carried Away

CALLED OUT OF A FACULTY MEETING in the spring of 1973, Stephen King drove home as fast as he could. As he had done every weekday since 1971, the 26-year-old King taught six classes of English at Hampden Academy, a small public school in Maine across the Penobscot River from Bangor. He carried a satchel full of student papers to read before he could turn to his real work—writing. A good teacher with a family to support, he earned just $6,400 per year, barely enough to sustain one person. Times were very hard.

In March, the Kings had been forced to cancel their telephone service because they could no longer afford it. So King's wife, Tabitha, had used a phone across the street from their home to call her husband and tell him that a telegram had arrived with news that would transform their lives.

The financial strain had begun to wear the Kings down. With their two small children, Naomi and Joseph, they lived in a rented trailer, and money was always tight. They had had to sublet one room in their already over-crowded home to King's childhood friend, Chris Chesley, to pay the rent.

Stephen King struggled financially before his first novel, *Carrie,* was published in 1973. King had originally thrown out the manuscript of *Carrie,* but his wife rescued the pages from the garbage and urged him to continue.

King and his wife had met five years earlier, when they were both students at the University of Maine at Orono. Everyone on campus recognized Stephen King, a tall, shambling figure who wrote a popular column called "King's Garbage Truck" for the campus newspaper. Most impressively, as an undergraduate he co-taught a course on popular culture. Politically active, he protested the Vietnam War and worked for civil rights. He and Tabitha, a history major, started dating after they met working in the stacks of the library during his junior and her sophomore year. The two had a lot in common—they had both grown up in Maine, and they were both writers. In 1970, King received his English degree and graduated with honors. They were married in January 1971, during her senior year. The future seemed promising for this bright young couple.

Stevens Hall housed the English department at the University of Maine at Orono in the late 1960s, when King attended the college. Upon King's graduation in 1970, he failed to find a job in which he would be able to use his English degree. Instead, King worked at a gas station and at a laundry.

But when King graduated, he discovered that an English degree did not automatically guarantee him employment. Too many other people with liberal arts educations were looking for work; the only job he could find was at a gas station. Soon he obtained another job at a laundry, earning $60 per week. Finally, he landed a teaching position where he could use his academic training, even if his salary was not enough to cover the bills. Tabitha went to work at Dunkin' Donuts, and King sometimes moonlighted at the laundry.

Nevertheless, King still held on to his childhood dream. When he was two years old, his father had disappeared. Stephen's mother, Nellie Ruth Pillsbury King, tried to support Stephen and his older brother, David, by herself. The family had to move frequently so she could find work, and they stayed with various relatives. Ruth King always worked several jobs at one time, and her only "vacations" were found in the pages of the books she read and treasured.

By age seven, Stephen King was writing. At first it was just for fun, but it soon became his dream to be a successful writer, and he became very disciplined and dedicated to writing.

After moving around a lot, his mother took 11-year-old Stephen and his brother back to Maine, where she had grown up, so she could care for her ailing parents. Stephen and David would live here until they went to college. It was at this time that King met Chris Chesley, a classmate, and they began to write together.

Since then, through all the hard times growing up, during college, and in the years he spent teaching, King always found time in every day—either early in the morning before he went to work, or late at night after the kids had gone to sleep—to spend a few hours writing. Those hours were difficult but the most compelling of the day. Piled on a shelf were more than 2,000 pages of unpublished manuscripts and a stack of rejection slips. But he believed in his potential as a writer, and his endeavors eventually did pull in some extra money.

Sometimes King was able to sell short stories to magazines. He would write a story, send it off to a magazine, and start writing the next story. If a magazine editor decided to publish a story, he still had to wait until it actually was in print before he received a check for his work. He counted on the checks to arrive just in time to "buy penicillin for one of the kids' ear infections or help meet the rent," paying off whatever bills demanded the most immediate attention.

The stress of their uncertain way of life took its toll. Sometimes King drank too much beer. Sometimes, sitting up with his sick, crying baby at three o'clock in the morning in the living room of the trailer, he wondered whether he would ever become a successful writer.

In 1972, King had sent several of his novels to publishers in New York City, who had rejected them. Occasionally, King had received some encouraging feedback from editors. One of his manuscripts was still at Doubleday for review, but he did not have high hopes for it. Actually, he disliked that particular novel.

The idea had seemed interesting at first. He had noticed that books like Ira Levin's *Rosemary's Baby* (1967) and William P. Blatty's *The Exorcist* (1970) had gotten a lot of attention, so he had tried to write his own supernatural horror novel instead of the usual naturalistic tales he wrote. He made some notes and began writing the story, but he got bored with it and threw the first few chapters in the trash. Tabitha, however, had fished the manuscript out of the garbage, read it, and told her husband that she really liked it and that he should try to finish it.

King took another look at the story. He had culled elements from his life to write it, from his high school days and his job as a teacher. There had been a strange, nerdy girl at his high school. She was overweight, had greasy hair and pimples, and did not talk to other people much. What had she really been like? he wondered. He began to write about her interior life. Then he added a twist to the plot. What if this lonely outcast had telekinetic powers? To fill out the story he added some realistic newspaper accounts, as if he had had a scrapbook of the media's investigation into the girl's story. This made the book longer and gave it an authentic flavor. He still did not like the manuscript, but he sent it to Doubleday anyway.

But as he drove his car home on that spring day in 1973 after his wife's phone call, none of his writing efforts seemed to matter. His family was barely surviving above the poverty line. The checks from the sales of his short stories were sporadic and could not be counted on, and recently he had taken on the additional responsibility of caring for his mother, who had cancer. He did not know what he could do to keep all their heads above water. Moreover, he was beginning to doubt that he would ever be taken seriously as a writer.

As he drove up to his family's trailer, Tabitha was waiting outside, holding an envelope. It was a telegram. Chesley stood in the doorway, watching. When King got out of the car he probably thought the telegram contained bad news because Tabitha was crying.

She ran up to him holding the telegram and told him that *Carrie*—his novel that he had detested so much—had been accepted for publication by Doubleday. King would be receiving an advance check for $2,500 within days.

King stood in front of his trailer and put his arms around his wife and cried. Chesley, who had known King for more than 10 years, looked on for a few minutes, then went back inside the trailer and tried to keep the kids

Carrie (actress Sissy Spacek) and Tommy (actor William Katt) are selected as King and Queen of the Bates High School prom in the 1976 movie *Carrie*. King's *Carrie*, a best-selling novel, was the first of his works to be made into a movie.

quiet while his two friends had a private moment of happiness together.

A month and a half later, on Mother's Day, King got a telephone call: Doubleday had sold the paperback rights to *Carrie* for $400,000. King received half of that amount. Within a few months, his whole life would change. He could resign from his teaching position—he enjoyed it and the students liked him, but he wanted to write full-time. He and his family could move out of their trailer and buy a house. But most of all, King wanted to do something special for Tabitha, who had stuck by him through the worst of times and had always encouraged him to keep writing. She had even rescued *Carrie* from the trash. He wanted to buy her a great present now that he had money to spend on her.

He walked around their small town for hours, looking in shop windows for the perfect present that would show his wife how much he appreciated her support and love. But his life had changed so quickly that he was totally overwhelmed—"freaked out," is how he phrased it. He could not concentrate. He shopped aimlessly, in a daze, and finally, he decided to buy her a hair dryer. It was not quite the gesture he had hoped to make, but Tabitha knew her husband, and he thought she would understand what he was trying to say.

Since 1973, King has published over 30 books, more than half of which have been made into movies. Today he is paid millions of dollars for each book he writes. A huge media storm accompanies every new Stephen King book that comes out—television and radio interviews, newspaper stories, reviews of the book, and even discussions about how much money he will receive in advance and how much in royalties. He rarely appears at book conventions anymore. If he does, he inevitably ends up being mobbed by fans.

Thousands of people line up for hours just for the privilege of seeing King or perhaps getting an autograph. It is impossible for him to sign as many as are requested— he gets tired after only 40 autographs. So he tends to remain secluded with his family in a big, rambling Victorian mansion—complete with a wrought-iron fence decorated with bats and spiders—in Bangor, Maine. He also owned a radio station, WZON in Bangor, where for a time he made sure rock music prevailed.

There is no doubt that King is enormously popular. He seems to have a profound effect on a variety of people. Many critics complain that his books are not "serious" and dismiss him as a blood-and-guts, gross-out type of horror writer. The bad reviews hurt him. But why would simple horror attract so much attention? The truth is, some of King's novels are fantasy stories, some are science fiction, and at least one is just a fairy tale. Even his most "horrible" novels are actually stories about real human relationships and how people operate in extreme circumstances.

Certain themes, like the lost father and the monstrous machine, occur and recur; train accidents often loom large. And King pays a great deal of attention to what goes on in his society: the assassination of President John F. Kennedy, nuclear accidents, toxic waste. One dedicated critic, Tony Magistrale, argues that "King's fiction . . . is contemporary social satire, revealing

King, photographed here in the 1970s, maintains that his novels are not merely horror tales but stories about real people and how they react in extreme circumstances. He takes readers out of the ordinary world and frightens them with his suggestions that the terrifying situations he creates could happen to them.

collective cultural fears and fantasies." His work reflects "the current maladies of our social relationships," especially "the narcissistic concern with the self . . . fostered by discontent with institutions." Social narcissism means being concerned only with one's own pleasures and performance, ignoring the social contract and the greater needs of society at large.

In King's work, the circumstances are a little bit more extreme than the average person might expect. For example, a winter storm might strand a family in a haunted hotel, and the father might begin to act strangely. Or a writer may suddenly discover he has an evil twin who is murdering everyone he ever knew. Or a devilishly charming old man might open an antique store that turns out to have human souls on its shelves. King concocts these bizarre and frightening situations, digging into his own secret fears to find them, and drops in regular people like his readers. Perhaps that is why his books sell so well: the reader sees how he or she might act in a situation with which—hopefully—he or she will never be confronted.

King still remembers how impressed he was as a child when he read *The Lion, the Witch and the Wardrobe,* one of the books in C. S. Lewis's Narnia series. The heroine, Lucy, goes into a closet and drops into another world. That is what King wants to do—drop readers out of the ordinary world—and he wants to scare people.

King's books are favorites worldwide. But King sees himself as a regular person who works hard for a living. He said in an interview, "For me, writing is like a little hole in reality that you can go through and you can get out and you can be somewhere else for a while. I live a very ordinary life. I have the children, and I have the wife—except for this thing that I do, this glitch, it's a very ordinary life."

2 ★ Growing Up

STEPHEN KING WAS BORN ON September 21, 1947. Two years later, his father, Donald Edwin King, went out for a pack of cigarettes and never came back home. He had married Nellie Ruth Pillsbury, who was called Ruth, in 1939, before he left with the merchant marine during World War II. Born in Peru, Indiana, to a family that had come from Ireland some years before, Donald King had very poor eyesight, a characteristic his son inherited. King describes his father in his critically acclaimed nonfiction book, *Danse Macabre,* as "a man of average height, handsome in a 1940's sort of way, a bit podgy, bespectacled."

Years later, Stephen King would find his father's legacy in his aunt Ethelyn's attic. Donald King had accumulated a large collection of paperback books, all fantasy and horror. He could always be found with a book, which when he was in the company of others he pretended was a Western. Stephen's father had wanted to be a writer, and he created many science fiction and horror short stories. None of Donald's stories were ever published, but Stephen did find a few encouraging rejection slips.

In this illustration from H. G. Wells's 1898 classic novel, *The War of the Worlds,* a man encounters a Martian as the creature's flying disk opens. The Wells story about Martians invading Earth was one of King's favorites as a child because it frightened him.

21

Ruth Pillsbury King told her son that she was distantly related to the well-known purveyors of instant crescent rolls, but theirs was a very distant relation indeed. She grew up in Maine; her father was a carpenter, and her mother was an intelligent, well-read housewife. Pillsbury played piano very well and had an eccentric sense of humor. She married Donald King in Croton-on-Hudson, New York, in 1939.

When Donald King returned from World War II in 1945, the couple adopted a boy, David, because Ruth's doctor said that she would never be able to bear children. The Kings moved to Maine, where Donald worked as a door-to-door salesman for various companies, including the Electrolux vacuum cleaner company. He began spending much of his time on the road for business. However, on September 21, 1947, much to the Kings' surprise, Stephen was born at Maine General Hospital in Portland.

Donald was spending more and more time away from home, and in 1949, when he left for good, Ruth had to raise her two small children by herself. The closest Ruth came to criticizing her errant husband was to say that he lacked sticking power.

Stephen King stated that his mother "landed on her feet, scrambling. Somehow she kept things together, as women before her have done and as other women are doing now as we speak." She began working a succession of low-wage jobs to support her family. They had to move often, as Ruth searched for better jobs, and they sometimes had to move in with other members of their family. At one time, Stephen King stayed with his aunt Ethelyn, one of his mother's sisters, in Durham, Maine, while David stayed with Molly, another maternal aunt, in Massachusetts. Their mother was forced to work elsewhere and could not keep the family together for this brief period, though she did visit both her sons.

When the boys and their mother were reunited, they moved to Chicago, Illinois, and lived with Donald King's parents, the Spanskys (Donald had changed his last name). Stephen was about three years old, and David was five. A year later they moved to De Pere, Wisconsin, where they lived in a house and got a dog. Their next move was to Fort Wayne, Indiana, where they stayed with Donald King's sister, Betty, who was a schoolteacher, and her friend Rudy. Finally, they got their own apartment, also in Fort Wayne, which David King says they shared with "a number of cockroaches."

The moves continued throughout Stephen's youth. Still, remembering those years, King says, "ours wasn't a

Merchant marines in training stand in formation on a ship in 1938, one year before the outbreak of World War II. Stephen's father, Donald King, was a captain in the U.S. merchant marine during the war. Stephen never knew his father; when Stephen was two years old Donald left home and never returned.

23

life of unremitting misery by any means, and we never missed a meal."

Ruth worked constantly, sometimes having two or three jobs at a time, and after her long days, she found rest and solace in romance novels. She also read to her sons, especially "Classics Comics," illustrated versions of great works of literature. Her favorites—and Stephen's—were the more frightening stories, such as H. G. Wells's *The Time Machine* and *The War of the Worlds,* and Robert Louis Stevenson's *The Strange Case of Dr. Jekyll and Mr. Hyde.*

When many years later in 1979 an interviewer asked King how he felt about children reading horror stories,

In this scene from the 1932 movie *Dr. Jekyll and Mr. Hyde,* the evil Mr. Hyde (right), played by Fredric March, looks sinisterly at a companion in a bar. The film was based on Robert Louis Stevenson's *The Strange Case of Dr. Jekyll and Mr. Hyde* (1886), one of the many books that King read when he was a boy.

his answer was: "I don't know. I did, and it warped me really good!" Presumably, this sense of being "warped" is part of King's background as a writer, something he approves of and cherishes.

According to his mother, when Stephen was four years old, he went out to play with a friend but returned sooner than expected, looking pale and shocked. Ruth asked him why he was home so soon, but he would not—or could not—speak for the rest of the day. Later that day, she found out that his friend had been run over by a freight train, possibly in Stephen's presence. Yet King has absolutely no memory of this accident.

Psychologists have speculated that King has been reliving the death of his friend in his subconscious ever since it happened, and that this explains King's fascination with the horror genre. King, however, disputes this theory. "I think that writers are made, not born or created out of dreams or childhood trauma, that becoming a writer . . . is a direct result of conscious will," he wrote in *Danse Macabre.*

Still, if the impulse is subconscious, he would not necessarily be aware that witnessing this accident is the reason for his fascination with horror. Although it is true that becoming a writer requires "conscious will," it is also true that not every writer chooses to write about the often gruesome subjects that King depicts. Despite King's denials, this early experience of seeing his friend die might have contributed greatly to his later writing. Certainly, accidents involving trains occur in a number of King's stories.

Some of King's dreams have worked their way into his fiction. In the chapter entitled "An Annoying Autobiographical Pause" in *Danse Macabre,* King reported one vivid nightmare that he had had at about age eight: "I saw the body of a hanged man dangling from the arm of a scaffold on a hill. This corpse bore a sign: ROBERT

BURNS. When the wind caused the corpse to turn in the air, I saw that it was my face—rotted and picked by the birds, but obviously mine. And then the corpse opened its eyes and looked at me." Sixteen years later, he used this dream, changing the name of the corpse to Hubie Marsten, as a central image in 'Salem's Lot.

Another dream recurs every so often in moments of stress and sends King shivering to Tabitha's side of the bed. As he describes in *Danse Macabre*:

> I am writing a novel in an old house . . . in a third floor room. A door on the far side communicates with the attic and I know—I know she [a homicidal maniac] is in there, and sooner or later the sound of my typewriter will cause her to come after me. She finally comes through the door . . . all gray hair and crazed eyes, wielding a meat ax. And when I run, I discover that somehow the house has . . . gotten ever so much bigger—and I'm totally lost.

King jokes that the madwoman in his attic might be a critic for the *New York Times Book Review*. He admits that bad reviews make painful reading. But he writes and talks about these dreams to make the important point that traumatic events do not make the writer. Instead, writers use material from all stages of their lives to create a successful finished work, but talented writers first work and study hard, then hone what they have observed, read, and dreamed into a shapely, well-paced narrative.

Throughout the King family's constant changes in location, Ruth managed to instill in her sons a strong Methodist background, always requiring them to attend church and Bible school. "There was a high premium on maintaining a pleasant exterior—saying 'please' and 'thank you' even if you're on the *Titanic* and it's going down, because that was the way you were supposed to behave," King told critic Douglas E. Winter in a 1982 interview.

As far back as King can remember, he was very inter-ested in good storytelling. Bible stories he first heard when he was six years old remain vivid. Other stories found their way into young Stephen's life, too; in 1953, two years after the incident in which his friend was killed, Stephen stood outside his mother's closed bedroom door as she listened to a Ray Bradbury story called "Mars Is Heaven!" on the radio.

In the radio drama, space travelers land on Mars and find themselves in what looks like their hometown—Greentown, Illinois. They are welcomed into the homes

Science fiction writer Ray Bradbury poses with space attire in a 1959 photograph. When King was six years old, he wanted to listen to a radio adaptation of Bradbury's story "Mars Is Heaven!" one night, but his mother would not allow it. Nevertheless, he listened to the story through his mother's closed bedroom door and afterward was so scared by what he had heard that he could not fall asleep.

of beloved parents, teachers, and sweethearts who have died; they celebrate. Only one space traveler remains quite rightly distrustful. For, in the night, the familiar faces melt away, and the travelers who thought they had found their way to heaven are all massacred.

Stephen crept back to his room and tried, unsuccessfully, to persuade his big brother to let him sleep in his bed for safety. He later wrote that, scared out of his wits, "I slept in the doorway, where the real and rational light of the bathroom bulb could shine on my face."

He considers himself the last of the generation that was spellbound by radio drama, a medium designed to rouse fear and trembling in its listeners as they imagined monsters far more terrifying than today's special effects that appear on a television or movie screen.

" 'A bug ten feet tall is pretty horrible,' the audience thinks, 'but I can deal with a ten-foot-bug. [In my imagination] I was afraid it might be a *hundred* feet tall,' " King wrote in "Radio and the Set of Reality," a chapter in *Danse Macabre*.

He also had great storytellers around him. As he describes in *Danse Macabre*:

> Some of the best yarns in those days were spun by my Uncle Clayton, a great old character who had never lost his childlike sense of wonder. Uncle Clayt would cock his hunting cap back on his mane of white hair . . . and launch into great stories, not only about ghosts but about local legends and scandals, family goings-on, the exploits of Paul Bunyan.

Not only could Uncle Clayton transport young Stephen into another world, but he could also "line bees." That is, Uncle Clayton could follow a bee back to the hive. He could also locate water by dowsing (using a divining rod that supposedly dips over the right spot when underground water is found). One dry summer, Uncle Clayton "magically" located a well, but the family did not have the money to drill for it. Years later when the Kings could afford to drill, the well came in just where Uncle Clayton said it would.

"Bone-skeptical" if credulous, King suspects that logical explanations exist for dowsing, but he quotes the saying of British scientist J. B. S. Haldane: "The universe is not only queerer than we suppose, but it is queerer than we *can* suppose."

Even as a child, King read voraciously. Among his absolute favorites was Robert Louis Stevenson's *The Strange Case of Dr. Jekyll and Mr. Hyde,* in which the good doctor is transformed by a magic potion into a homicidal monster. King remembers an incident in second grade, when his teacher caught him reading a book by Jack London in class. The book was *The Call of the Wild,* generally considered to be difficult material for a seven-year-old. Certainly his teacher thought so; she accused him of only pretending to read, and kept him after school. King had to read the book aloud to prove he could do it. Of course, he passed her test.

It is hard to imagine the husky, tall man that King is today ever having had a sick day in his life, but King was often ill during his childhood. He was even out of school for an entire year, bedridden. During these times, he had plenty of opportunity to read, and he also started to write. He began by copying some of the stories that he read, and then he became motivated to write his own stories. One of the earliest was about dinosaurs taking over the world, which was much like the simplistic adventure stories he was reading at the time. A scientist discovers that the dinosaurs are allergic to leather (an idea that has no basis in fact, but bear in mind, King was only seven years old at the time), and the townspeople throw all their leather coats, car seats, boots, and saddles at the dinosaurs. The dinosaurs run away. A clever story, it shows that King thought about storytelling at a very early age.

In the 1954 film *The Creature from the Black Lagoon,* the half-man, half-fish creature seen here is discovered by scientists near the Amazon River. Although the seven-year-old Stephen knew that the creature in the movie was not real, the monster still terrified him. King believes today that children are the best audience for the genre of horror because they can easily suspend disbelief.

King still remembers seeing his first horror movie, *The Creature from the Black Lagoon,* at a drive-in theater. One scene still haunts him—the monster, slowly but surely, walls in the idyllic hero and heroine, as they cavort, innocent and unaware, in a lovely pool.

Even at age seven, King knew that the creature was not real. Nonetheless, it became ingrained in his mind. It visited his dreams, waited in the closet, lurked in the bathroom at the end of the dark hall. He was the perfect audience for horror movies.

In fact, King thinks children are the perfect audience for horror films because they do not make sharp distinctions between reality and the imagination. They can suspend disbelief. They might know that the dead woman who suddenly comes after Danny in *The Shining* is really an actress earning her salary, but they scream because they are as frightened as they would be if they were the pursued.

The "willing suspension of disbelief," which the English poet Samuel Taylor Coleridge talked about, is how audiences accept poetry, fantasy, or any work of the imagination. Disbelief, King says, is very heavy, "a lead weight." He feels some sympathy for people who tell him they dismiss fantasy, science fiction, and horror because they are not real. "The muscles of the imagination" have grown too flabby. They are simply too weak to "lift the weight of imagination."

Kids may be small, but "they are the jugglers of the invisible world," accepting with ease talking trees, mice in tuxedos, and fat Santas who slide down narrow chimneys. And horror stories, like fairy tales, give children and adults ways to handle and come to terms with their fears.

Always interested in monsters, as a child King devoured *Fate,* an occultist magazine. He sees that his attraction to horror stories has a solid psychological basis. His childhood nightmares were inadequacy dreams, "standing up to salute the flag and having my pants fall down" or getting to class unprepared. Without a father, he needed his "own power trips." His alter ego as a child was the made-up daredevil Cannonball Cannon, a hero who "did good deeds" at home and in the West.

In a June 1983 *Playboy* interview with Eric Norden, King described himself as "prey to a lot of conflicting emotions as a child." Despite having friends, Stephen "often felt unhappy and different." Buck-toothed with thick glasses, "I was a fat kid—husky was the euphemism they used in the clothing store—and pretty poorly coordinated, always the last picked when we chose [sports] teams."

There were compensations. Stephen King began his lifelong love of rock-and-roll music early. His first record, a Christmas gift from his mother, included Elvis Presley's "Hound Dog" on one side and "Don't Be Cruel" on the other. He played that 78 rpm until the grooves were worn down. Discovering rock and roll meant "finding something that was very, very powerful. It made you bigger than you were . . . tough even if you weren't tough. I just love rock and roll," King told Mat Schaffer in an October 31, 1983, radio interview. King still plays the guitar, and he remains as committed to rock and roll as ever.

When King was 10 years old, his family lived in Stratford, Connecticut, where King came to a realization that he has said was a turning point in his life. On October 4, 1957, he attended a Saturday matinee of *Earth vs. the Flying Saucers,* a mediocre science fiction film, which was not particularly frightening, but King remembers it vividly because the projectionist stopped the screening midreel and the house lights came on. The theater manager came out, stood in front of the blank movie screen, and announced that the Soviet Union, which was an enemy superpower of the United States's at the time, had successfully launched a space satellite, *Sputnik I,* into orbit. Then the lights went down, and the Technicolor monsters on-screen continued their attack on humankind.

This may not seem like a cataclysmic event today, when so many countries have satellites in orbit and the United States has sent people to the moon many times over. But in 1957, the United States and the Soviet Union were locked in a standoff called the cold war, both racing for technical superiority. As King describes it, he was "a member of that entire generation of war

On October 4, 1957, the Soviet Union launched the first space satellite, *Sputnik I*, a replica of which is shown here. The fact that the chief rival of the United States had managed to get ahead of them in the "space race" shocked and frightened most Americans. King remembers the news of *Sputnik*'s launch as the time when his innocence was lost.

babies . . . reared smug in the myth of America's military invincibility and moral supremacy." The idea that the Soviet Union could have beaten the United States in the race into space was terrifying. At that moment, the imaginary horror of his childhood became the reality of an adult world where his way of life really could be threatened. He remembers it as one of the most frightening and depressing moments of his life, the moment when his innocence was lost.

3 The Maine Years

IN 1958, WHEN STEPHEN WAS 11 and David was 13, Ruth King realized that her parents, Guy Pillsbury and Nellie Fogg Pillsbury, who were in their eighties and in poor health, needed help. Her sisters offered Ruth an arrangement: they would all help her out financially if she would move into the modest farmhouse down a dirt road in Durham, Maine's western section, known as Methodist Corner. She would aid their ailing parents, acting as a nurse-caretaker.

Caring for the two invalids would not be an easy job, but Ruth would lovingly tend to her parents, and the family would settle down in a town they already knew well. Stephen had been spending his summers there with his aunt and uncle, and now he and David could go to school without fear of having to move before the end of the year. At last they could put down roots and live a more stable life. Ruth and her sons moved into the little house in Durham, a small working-class town.

Stephen attended classes in a one-room schoolhouse. His teacher described him as "a smart, friendly, outgoing boy" who was always writing. He attended

This picture of Stephen King appeared in the Lisbon High School yearbook in 1966, the year he graduated. An above-average student, King played on the football team, performed in a rock-and-roll band, and wrote for the school newspaper.

the old Methodist church next to his house and taught Bible school as a teenager during summer vacations.

Years later, in a 1983 interview with Eric Norden, King said, "For ten years, we lived a virtual barter existence, practically never seeing any hard cash. If we needed food, relatives would bring a bag of groceries; if we needed clothes, there'd always be hand-me-downs."

In the summers, the well went dry, and water had to be trucked in. The house also had no indoor plumbing. Stephen and David had to walk to their aunt's house for baths, and if Stephen needed to go to the bathroom in the middle of the night, he had to make his way across a dark backyard to the blue outhouse. King always was and still is afraid of the dark.

"I suffered from any number of irrational fears," he admits. Stefan Kanfer, who interviewed King for a *Time* cover story in October 1986 listed King's fears as "spiders, elevators, closed-in places, the dark, sewers, funerals, the idea of being buried alive, cancer, heart attacks, the number 13, black cats and walking under ladders." King reasons that his fears stem from the fact that he was and is "unreservedly credulous."

The introduction to *Nightmares & Dreamscapes,* the most recent collection of his short stories, begins, "When I was a kid I believed everything I was told, everything I read, and every dispatch sent out by my own overheated imagination." The last on his block to decide that "those street-corner Santas meant there was no *real* Santa," King accepted his uncle's assertion that you could tear a person's shadow with a steel tent-peg and his aunt's belief that shivering meant a goose had just walked over your eventual grave.

And he believed school-yard yarns even when they contradicted themselves. Somehow, simultaneously, he managed to believe that a dime left on a railroad track would derail a train and that the same dime left on a track

A view from Acadia National Park on Mt. Desert Island shows part of Maine's rugged coast. King has spent most of his life in Maine and chooses to set his novels and short stories in fictional Maine towns that are much like the places where he grew up.

would expand to the size of a half-dollar, albeit a transparently thin one.

King wrote that his "primary sources of wonderful and amazing facts in those days were the paperback compilations from *Ripley's Believe It or Not!*" Ripley's curiosities were real to King, teaching him "how fine the line between the fabulous and the humdrum could sometimes be."

Despite their poverty, King told sports announcer Mel Allen, his mother "was determined that David and I would go to college. She always told us that dreams and ambitions can cause bitterness if they're not realized, and she encouraged me to submit my writings."

Around 1960, Stephen and David made a discovery that would change their lives. On a chilly autumn day in the attic over their aunt and uncle's garage, the boys discovered a box filled with possessions their father had left behind. Inside were memorabilia from the merchant marine, including scrapbooks, manuals, and the maritime uniform Donald had worn, as well as Super 8 movie reels. The brothers rented a movie projector and watched films of their father taken sometime during World War II. There was also some color footage of Donald King standing on the deck of a ship waving. Both David and Stephen have said that they still feel some anger toward their absent father, but they do not seem to think about him often.

Another box proved even more precious: it contained a treasure trove of paperback books—horror tales—and Stephen proceeded to read every one of them. In particular, King remembers books by H. P. Lovecraft, a popular horror writer of the twenties and thirties, as well as other stories from *Weird Tales* magazine. Stephen had seen horror movies, but they were B movies (low-budget) and hard to take seriously. He was struck by the sincerity of these books. Not just silly camp, horror was something that could be done well and that could really scare people. His mother told him that his father had written stories and tried to have them published. Stephen found rejection slips, some of which were encouraging, but none of Donald's work had survived. Stephen had been writing stories since he was seven without even suspecting that his father had written them, too.

In 1959, Stephen met Chris Chesley, another creative young man who shared his interest in reading good stories and trying to write them. They met at the one-room school that they both attended, where King was a grade ahead of Chesley. Chesley was immediately interested in this intelligent 12-year-old who, as Chesley says, "already had a way with words." King showed Chesley some of the stories he had written, and Chesley was greatly impressed. The writing was better than any published work he had ever seen by a contemporary author.

This illustration appears on the book jacket of a collection of H. P. Lovecraft's stories, entitled *The Horror in the Museum,* and depicts a creepy skeleton crawling out of a chasm. In their aunt's attic, Stephen and his brother, David, found a box left by their father that was full of books, including some by H. P. Lovecraft, a popular horror writer of the 1920s and '30s. King once described Lovecraft, who was a powerful influence on King, as "the best writer of horror fiction that America has yet produced."

The two began writing stories together. Sometimes they would take turns writing paragraphs, while at other times they would each write their own stories and then give them to each other to critique. They also read aloud to each other from their favorite books, such as Richard Matheson's *I Am Legend* and Don Robertson's *The River and the Wilderness.*

Meanwhile, David had acquired an old Underwood typewriter and a mimeograph machine that had to be cranked by hand. He began publishing a local newspaper called *Dave's Rag,* with a staff consisting of him, his cousin Donald Flaws, and his younger brother, Stephen. David was editor-in-chief, Donald was the sports editor, and Stephen was a general reporter. The boys included everything that they thought would be of interest in the town of Durham, from church news to people's birthdays to local renovations.

In imitation of *Mad* magazine, the top right corner of *Dave's Rag* announced the price: "5 cents—cheap!" They later increased the price to 20 cents. If readers wanted a copy of a photograph taken by David that appeared in the newspaper, they could buy it for 35 cents. And if local businesses wanted to advertise their wares, it would cost them two cents per line for a classified ad.

Stephen King's contributions to *Dave's Rag* varied. In one column he gave readers a preview of the new shows that would be coming on television. He went to movies and provided reviews and synopses of their plots. He also published his first short stories in the paper, copies of which readers could also buy directly from him.

King's grandmother, Nellie Fogg Pillsbury, died at the age of 85, "blind and bedridden, but still able to decline Latin verbs and name all of the Presidents up to Truman." Fourteen-year-old Stephen was the one to find her body after she died in her sleep. He did not know what to do. He had seen people in movies hold a mirror up to a dead person's mouth to make sure there was no breath, so this is what he did to verify that she was indeed dead. He would use this material in a short story, "Gramma," printed first in the semiprofessional magazine *Weirdbook*, issue number 19, in spring 1984, and reprinted in *Skeleton Crew*, a 1985 collection of his short stories.

Real evil also fascinated King. He kept a scrapbook documenting the murders committed in cold blood by Charles Starkweather in January 1958. Starkweather and his girlfriend, Caril Fugate, went on a killing spree through the states of Nebraska and Wyoming. "I loved the guy," King said. "At the same time, he scared me." King claims that his mother was ready to have him placed in analysis. He used that material in the short story "The Revenge of Lard Ass Hogan," which appeared in the *Maine Review* in 1975, and in another short story, "Nona" in 1978. "The Revenge of Lard Ass Hogan" was revised and reprinted in the novella "The Body," appearing as a story written by the character Gordon Lachance, which had purportedly been published in *Cavalier*, a magazine that printed King's early stories. In 1986, "The Body" was made into the movie *Stand By Me*.

Stephen graduated from grammar school at the top of his class, which consisted of just three students. There was no high school in Durham, so the eight eligible students were sent to Lisbon Falls, a nearby town. Because there was no bus, the town paid a service to drive the students to and from high school every day. If Stephen stayed late for an activity and missed the cars that left for home, he would hitchhike or walk the six miles back to Durham.

A girl who commuted to high school with young Stephen was one of the people on whom, some years later, he would model the character Carrie for the novel of the same name. Nobody wanted to be stuck sitting next to the pimply, nerdy girl in the crowded backseat of the car.

Religion played a major part in the Kings' lives. Because their church could not afford a full-time minister, occasionally Stephen preached the Sunday sermon. Charles Huff, a lay minister and a retired postmaster, and "the world's worst driver," according to David King, drove the boys to camp meetings as well. Huff had "a profound impact" on both boys, according to David. When he passed away, Stephen delivered a eulogy for "Huffy."

In 1962, at age 15, Stephen began submitting his short stories to science fiction magazines. He did not meet with much success. In fact, he had a huge pile of rejection slips

Wil Wheaton (left), River Phoenix (center), Jerry O'Connell (pointing), and Corey Feldman (right), star as four boys who search for the body of a missing youth in the 1986 movie *Stand By Me*. The film, directed by Rob Reiner, was based on King's partly autobiographical novella, "The Body."

that he speared on a nail on his desk. He was proud of his collection of rejections; it showed he was trying, anyway, and paying his dues.

Stephen did well in high school. In his free time, he played in a rock band and was on the football team. He also started an underground newspaper, the *Village Vomit,* a satirical version of the school paper, where he mocked teachers and administrators. He got in trouble for that, but the principal, seeing that he had potential, arranged for him to write about high school sports for the local newspaper.

Another odd thing he did was write detailed stories about his high school and the people in it, but he put his acquaintances in extraordinary circumstances. For instance, in one story, the school was attacked by the Soviet army, and the students fought back. Friends who appeared as characters in his stories knew Stephen liked them if they were among the last to go or if they died gloriously.

According to Chris Chesley, "Steve's characters are based not only upon the horror genre tradition but also on actual people he has known." Chesley has said that King was fashioned by his "working class, gritty little town. A lot of the narrative force in his writing stems directly from his sense of being outside the mainstream, outside the middle class ethos [values]."

In 1963, Chris and Stephen published an 18-page anthology of their short stories called *People, Places, and Things* using the typewriter and the mimeograph machine that Stephen's brother had used to put together his newspaper a few years back. They sold it to friends and family. And in 1965, King had "I Was a Teenage Grave Robber" published in an actual magazine—*Comics Review.* He did not get paid for this short story, but at last he could point to a story he had written that was actually published.

4 "A Marketable Obsession"

STEPHEN KING HAD BEEN OFFERED a partial scholarship to Drew University in Madison, New Jersey, a prestigious school with Methodist affiliations, but the family still could not afford it, which did not bother him because he had always preferred Maine to just about anywhere else.

In 1966, King began college at the University of Maine at Orono, where he majored in English, minored in drama, and quickly became a campus icon. Both he and his brother, David, got scholarships and took whatever part-time jobs they could get to support their education.

King told Mel Allen that his mother would "send us $5 nearly every week for spending money. After she died, I found she had frequently gone without meals to send that money we'd so casually accepted. It was very unsettling."

Fellow students remember King as a big, hulking figure with a wild beard and untamed hair who would never win the best-dressed award. He wrote a column, "King's Garbage Truck," in the university newspaper, which he used as a political mouthpiece. One editor of the *Maine Campus* said, "King was always late. We would be pulling our hair out at deadline. Steve would come

Stephen King delivers the commencement address to the class of 1987 at his alma mater, the University of Maine at Orono. Seventeen years earlier, King graduated from the university, where he majored in English and minored in drama.

in and sit down at a typewriter and produce two flawless pages of copy. He carries stories in his head the way most people carry change in their pockets."

As the final examination for a course in Gothic literature that he took in his sophomore year, King could choose to write either a term paper or a short piece of Gothic fiction. Gothic fiction, prevalent in the late 18th century and early 19th century, is a literary style that stresses grotesque, mysterious, and melancholic themes. King produced "Jerusalem's Lot," later published in *Night Shift*, his 1978 collection of short stories, and an early draft of one of King's favorite novels, *'Salem's Lot*. Though the professor had warned his students that his standards for fiction were very high, "Jerusalem's Lot" earned King an A, which King said he did not deserve. "The story," he said, "wasn't so much Gothic as it was outrageous Lovecraft pastiche [imitation]." In "Jerusalem's Lot," set in 1850, Charles Boone travels back to a deserted Maine town where he discovers that his ancestors worshiped vampires, the undead. The last of his kind, he chooses to end his life to rid the world of their dreadful practices.

King switched political allegiances when he got to college. In high school he was a conservative Republican who believed in the government and the status quo. He voted for Richard Nixon for president because he believed Nixon would end the war in Vietnam. Tabitha claims that he was absurdly naive, King reports in the introductory chapter of *Nightmares & Dreamscapes*. "My wife still delights in telling people that her husband cast his first Presidential ballot, at the tender age of twenty-one for Richard Nixon. 'Nixon said he had a plan to get us out of Vietnam,' she says, usually with a gleeful gleam in her eye, *'and Steve believed him!'* "

But in college, as he watched America become increasingly involved in Vietnam, he became more and more

liberal and even radical. He rallied against the war and also involved himself in civil rights causes.

In 1966, his freshman year, his short story "The Glass Floor" was accepted for publication by *Startling Mystery Stories,* a semiprofessional science fiction magazine. This was the first story for which King actually received money. He also completed a dystopian (depressingly wretched and involving people who lead a fearful existence) novel, *The Long Walk,* which he submitted to a first-novel contest. Set in the future, the novel follows a group of teenagers on a long journey during which they are killed one by one. Crushed by the standard rejection letter, King packed the manuscript away without showing it to any other publishers.

This photograph, taken around 1963, shows the sprawling campus of the University of Maine at Orono. When King attended college there, he was a campus icon widely known for his column "King's Garbage Truck" in the university newspaper, the *Maine Campus.*

King submitted the novel he completed in his sophomore year to a dozen publishers, and it was rejected by all of them. Interestingly, when he took classes in creative writing, they interfered with his productivity. King called the classes "a constipating experience" and "the worst thing I could have done to myself." He told Douglas E. Winter, "it really muffled everything for awhile."

Strong positive influences were such realist and naturalist writers as Thomas Hardy, Jack London, and Theodore Dreiser, who carefully document every detail of scene and character. King says he wants his readers to know that they always walk into the middle of a story; that is, that everything and everyone has histories. When

King jumps into a story, he wants to tell readers what has already happened to everyone before the tale begins.

A poetry seminar taught by Burton Hatlen focused on contemporary American mythology and taught King that he could bridge the gulf between academic and popular culture. Hatlen read and admired King's work, as did Ted Holmes, who taught creative writing. But King had running battles with other professors "who sneered at the popular fiction I carried around all the time."

But popular authors taught King a lot about plotting and pace. According to King, his muse was definitely not "some cute little pudgy devil who floats around the head of the creative person sprinkling fairy dust." King de-

On May 4, 1970, at Kent State University, Ohio, National Guardsmen shot tear gas and fired rifles into the masses demonstrating against the war in Southeast Asia, killing four students and wounding several more. In high school, King had been a conservative Republican, but in his college years, during the late 1960s, he became increasingly radical and fought for civil rights causes and rallied against the Vietnam War.

scribes his muse as "a guy with a flattop in coveralls who looks like Jack Webb [the actor who starred in the 1960s television show "Dragnet"] and says, 'All right, you son of a bitch, time to get to work.'"

A number of King's short stories appeared in college literary magazines. One story, "It Grows On You," which originally appeared in a University of Maine literary magazine, *Marshroots,* was revised and republished in the most recent collection of King's short stories, *Nightmares & Dreamscapes.* The story is now "a final look back at the doomed little town of Castle Rock [the fictional town that is the setting of many of King's novels]."

The Accident, a one-act play, won a drama award from the university, and a number of other stories that King wrote in college would resurface later. "Stud City," first published in the fall 1969 issue of *Ubris,* a campus literary magazine, reappears in "The Body," where it supposedly is the early work of the character Gordon Lachance, who criticizes it. He calls it "derivative and sophomoric," all too clearly "THE PRODUCT OF AN UNDERGRADUATE CREATIVE WRITING WORKSHOP."

In 1969, King began talking to various professors and administrators about an idea he had for a course on popular literature and culture. The world had changed so much in the sixties—since the forties, really—and now there was a huge amount of information, entertainment, and music that no one was studying. Administrators did not think it was a serious enough topic to warrant study in an academic institution. King was persistent, however, and eventually he ended up teaching the course. Officially, he was a teaching assistant, and a full professor was in charge.

While in college, King met Tabitha Spruce, a history major from Old Town, Maine. The third of eight children, Tabitha had wanted to study archaeology and history at the University of New Mexico but could not

An artist's sketch of Theodore Dreiser depicts the novelist in 1938. Dreiser, who is considered by most critics to be the pioneer of naturalism in American literature, wrote his most acclaimed novel, *An American Tragedy,* in 1925. While in college, King was introduced to the works of prominent authors such as Dreiser, who greatly influenced his writing.

afford to attend the school. Like King, she landed at the university library, working part-time in the stacks. They began dating and were soon a couple. According to King, "Tabby looked like a waitress. She came across—and still does—as a tough broad."

Tabitha Spruce has French-Canadian forebears who, she says, changed their name from Pinette, which means "Little Pine," to Spruce, an American tree. They used the new name to disguise their Roman Catholicism from the local Ku Klux Klan, a secret society that began terrorizing Catholics, among other religious and racial groups, in the late 19th century.

Wearing a borrowed suit that was too big for him, King married Tabitha in January 1971, soon after his graduation. Tabitha completed her degree in history a year later.

His final column for "King's Garbage Truck" in the *Maine Campus* was a caricature birth announcement: Stephen King had been born into the "real" world. That summer he contributed weekly installments of a comic Western novel, *Slade,* to the campus newspaper. Slade, a two-gun cigar smoker swathed in black who has lost his sweetheart, Miss Polly Peachtree of Paduka, triumphs over various villains and rides off into the sunset in search of new adventures. King himself would have a rather more difficult time of it.

Artist Max Beerbohm's caricature of Thomas Hardy shows the English novelist and poet composing a lyric. Hardy, whose work impressed King, was a realist in his portrayal of details and a naturalist in his philosophic outlook. His novels, such as *The Mayor of Casterbridge* and *Tess of the D'Urbervilles,* take place in fictional Wessex in southwestern England and involve simple country folk.

When King graduated from college, the working world was not very receptive to a recent graduate with a degree in English. King worked a variety of jobs, including pumping gas for $1.25 per hour. Soon he was able to switch to a higher-paying job, such as pressing sheets at the New Franklin Laundry in Bangor for $1.60 an hour.

In one of his early stories, "The Mangler," an automatic ironing and folding machine turns into a murderous satanic monster, stalking the countryside, searching for victims. That industrial speed ironer is very much like the machines King operated when he worked at the laundry. Also, in *Carrie* the creepy mother works at a laundry. In other words, no experience of King's is wasted—he may have hated that job, but he found something to use during those hours, and he turned it into a story, then used it in a book.

The Kings moved into a rented trailer. In May 1971, after she graduated, Tabitha put on a hot-pink uniform and began working at Dunkin' Donuts. Their daughter, Naomi, born within the first year of their marriage, was dressed mostly in scrounged clothes. And on June 4, 1972, their second child, Joseph, was born.

In 1971, King landed a teaching job at Hampden Academy, where he had been a student teacher during his senior year of college. His salary of $6,400 per year was not much more than he had earned at the laundry. He went back to work at the laundry during the summer break. Times were really hard, but King managed to make good use of his surroundings, no matter how uncongenial. For example, he began to wonder what the children of a co-worker at the laundry, an extremely religious older woman with "a strange aura," were like. She became the prototype for Carrie's mother in that novel.

Even though there was precious little room in their tiny trailer, the Kings took in Stephen's childhood friend,

Chris Chesley, as a boarder. King said, "Budget was not exactly the word for whatever it was we were on. . . . It was more like a modified version of the Bataan Death March [the infamous 65-mile death march of American and Filipino prisoners of war from Bataan, a peninsula in the Philippines, to Japanese prison camps during World War II]."

Through it all, King continued to write, working for two hours every night in the furnace room of their trailer, Tabitha's typewriter perched on a child's rickety desk or on his lap. When he got excited the desk jiggled up and down. King would "go down there and fight vampires" at will. He had started writing a book, *The Dark Tower,* and his short stories occasionally brought in a little money—just in time, usually.

He had a dartboard on which he could post rejection slips. "When I was really feeling down I used to throw darts at them and I would say, 'There, that's for you, *Cosmopolitan.* Take that, *Alfred Hitchcock!'* " He points out that writers need thick skins.

Noting a horror trend that began with *Rosemary's Baby* (1967) and included *The Exorcist* (1970), King began writing *Carrie* in the summer of 1972 but tossed the notes in the trash; Tabitha rescued the pages and told him to continue. He hated it, but he finished the book and sent it to a publisher anyway. His expectations were low; he had gotten many, many rejections.

In the novel, Carrie, the plain daughter of a religious fanatic, is tormented by her high school classmates. Her experience of puberty is so harrowing that she develops paranormal powers and takes cataclysmic revenge upon her tormentors.

Then the telegram arrived—*Carrie* was to be published! And King would receive a $2,500 advance. A month and a half later, on May 12, 1973, King got an astonishing phone call. His publisher, Doubleday, had

During his junior year in college, King began dating fellow student Tabitha Jane Spruce, shown here in a later photograph. They had met while working in the university's library and were married January 2, 1971. Years later, King wrote, "The only important thing I ever did in my life for a conscious reason was to ask Tabitha Spruce . . . to marry me."

55

sold the paperback rights for $400,000, of which Stephen King got half.

The Kings' lives could have changed immediately and dramatically. But they took things one step at a time. First, they moved to a modest apartment in Bangor, where King thought about whether or not to give up teaching. He was a popular teacher and liked his job, but he finally decided to resign and dedicate himself to writing full time. The family then moved to Windham, near Sebago Lake, where King could fish and spend the summer writing his next book, with occasional forays into New York to see his publisher and take in a baseball game. King is an avid fan of the Boston Red Sox.

The book, initially titled "Second Coming," then "Jerusalem's Lot," would eventually appear as *'Salem's Lot* in 1975 and would be nominated for Best Novel in the World Fantasy Awards the next year.

From then on he would write every day, 362 days per year. King takes vacation days on his birthday, Christ-

Stephen King speaks to children at the Waterford Memorial School in Waterford, Maine, in 1990. King was familiar with the classroom—in 1971 he began teaching at Hampden Academy, near Bangor, where the school's principal later said "King was a promising teacher." He resigned from this position in 1973 to dedicate his time to writing.

mas, and the Fourth of July. "I have a marketable obsession," he tells his readers in the foreword to *Night Shift,* a 1978 collection of his short stories.

He attributes his success at least in part to his mother's partaking of America's national habit: worrying. "I was brought up by a mom who worried all the time. She'd say, 'Put on your rubbers, Stevie, you'll get a cold. You're gonna get pneumonia and die.' You couldn't go swimming in public pools because of polio and stuff like that." Worry, King says, is "a luxury we can afford," because we are a rich nation, "the best educated nation on earth. We have everything."

Actor Max von Sydow (right) presents author and producer William Blatty (left) and actress Linda Blair (center) with Golden Globe awards for their work on the 1973 movie *The Exorcist.* Upon realizing that horror novels, like Blatty's *The Exorcist,* were getting much attention during this time, King decided to write one himself.

King's hardworking, beloved mother lived long enough to hear the good news of the publication of *Carrie,* but not long enough to hold the book in her hand. On December 18, 1973, Ruth died at age 59, after a long and painful battle with cancer. One of King's greatest regrets is that his mother, who encouraged him so much to write throughout his childhood, did not live to see *Carrie* actually in print. He told radio announcer Mel Allen, "she was old-fashioned about *Carrie.* She didn't like the sex parts. But she recognized that a lot of *Carrie* had to do with bullying. If there's a moral in the book it is 'Don't mess around with people. You never know whom you may be tangling with.'" King added, "Ah, if my mother had lived, she'd have been the Queen of Durham by now."

5 King of Horror

IN 1974, ANXIOUS TO TRY NEW SETTINGS, King moved his family to Boulder, Colorado, where he thought he could seclude himself and write. While living there he heard of an old resort and decided to go there for a short visit. He and his family stayed at the Stanley Hotel, where according to fable, Johnny Ringo, a local legendary bad man, had been shot. King had to pay the bill in cash because the hotel had closed for the season. "We were the only guests," King said, "and we could hear the wind screaming outside." When they went down to supper, they walked "through these big bat-wing doors into a huge dining room." Plastic sheets covered the tables, and chairs were stacked up on them. A band dressed in tuxedos played, but the place was empty. On the way back to his room, King got lost in the warren of dark corridors. When he found his room, he went into the bathroom and looked

---

In 1974, King and his family temporarily moved to Boulder, Colorado, where King wrote *The Shining*. He believed Colorado was an ideal locale for a horror novel, because, he said, it is "a spooky state with mountains and high passes and the wind howling and the wolves."

at the claw-foot tub and thought, "What if somebody died here? At that moment, I knew I had a book."

That visit to the Stanley Hotel in Estes Park, which began the day before Halloween, would provide the plot and setting for *The Shining* (1977), originally titled "The Shine," from a song by John Lennon and the Plastic Ono Band called "Instant Karma": "We all shine on, like the moon and the stars and the sun."

In just over a month, King wrote the major part of *The Shining* in a rented room because there was no space to work at the house in which the Kings lived in Boulder. He paid $17.50 per week to a landlady he had seen once, leaving the check on the counter. All he knew when he started writing his novel was that it would be five acts, "in the form of a Shakespearean tragedy." He said that he "just never hit a snag in the whole writing of the book."

While in Boulder, he also began working on *The House on Value Street,* a novel loosely based on the true story of newspaper heiress Patty Hearst's February 1974 kidnapping by the Symbionese Liberation Army (SLA), her brainwashing, and her apparent participation in a bank robbery. Though the real-life drama seemed to have all the elements for great nonfiction, King felt that fiction might better be able to explain all of the contradictions. The themes and material would eventually resurface in *The Stand,* arguably his most popular work, but no matter how hard King tried, he could not make *Value Street* work. He dropped the book.

Like the doomed Jack Torrance of *The Shining,* who can only type over and over again, "All work and no play makes Jack a dull boy," King has had serious bouts of writer's block, which he calls "a mental constipation." In a radio interview recorded in 1992, he said, "When I can't work, I tell myself it will pass. I am compulsive. If I don't write, a voice inside agitates for the work. If you don't use it, you'll lose it. I've had periods when I've written nothing but crap for as long as a year."

King is usually amazingly prolific, producing one or two best-sellers a year, as well as movie and television scripts and solid advice for novice writers. He rewrites his books three or four times, though "most of what you want should be there" the first time around. He tells stories about real, not cardboard, characters, people his audience cares about. In the second draft, he goes back and fixes whatever is wrong.

"The second draft is especially critical," he told critic Tony Magistrale in a 1989 interview, because often "a writer is unaware of what he's really writing until after he is done. It's like drawing pictures in a dark room, and then a sudden illumination shows you what you've been drawing. Before you write it down, the story exists, but it takes the actual writing to recognize it." He often finds that the second half of a book teaches him what the book is really about, and he must revise the earlier sections so that they lead more naturally to the end.

"On the third draft I concentrate on language and make the sentences feel balanced. Good writing should be accessible." King gets fan mail from kids who do not usually read at all, let alone write letters. "Labored, almost scrawled things in pencil, they say, I don't read much, but I love what you do," King told interviewer David Stevens. An inveterate reader who believes a day without a book is a total waste, King is pleased that these readers gain confidence and sharpen their skills by reading his stories. The story grabs them, and despite the difficulty, they read on to find out what happens next. With their newfound assurance, "they go on from there."

Within a year of moving to Colorado, King returned to Maine—where he has always felt most at home—and bought a house in Bridgton. His second novel, a particular favorite of his, 'Salem's Lot, was published in 1975,

In 1975, King published his second novel, *'Salem's Lot,* which is a modern-day vampire story set in a New England town. With the publication of this novel, King's editor, Bill Thompson, was worried that King would be typecast as a horror writer.

hitting the best-seller list and proving that *Carrie* was not a fluke.

A vampire story set in Jerusalem's Lot, a small New England town, the novel reverses the traditional American hate affair with cities. This time, the small town, usually a place of peace and quiet, is the site of malevolence. Readers of *'Salem's Lot* sometimes believe that King himself hates small towns, but in a 1979 interview he told Mel Allen that though the novel shows the defects, the negative side of middle-class America, "much of it is a love song to growing up in a small town."

King acknowledges the influence of his beloved horror movies on this novel, especially the paranoia that informs *Invasion of the Body Snatchers.* The movie responded to the witch-hunts of Senator Joseph McCarthy, who was chairman of the special Senate investigating committee that insisted that communism had infested the country, smearing numerous citizens by innuendo. The paranoia of *'Salem's Lot,* King says, is a parallel response to the Watergate scandal, the Republican break-in at the Democratic campaign headquarters that led to the eventual resignation of President Richard Nixon. He also found the ending of *Invasion* quite romantic: the last two uncontaminated humans, the lovers, are wrapped in one another's arms as the podpeople, who once were their neighbors, close in on them.

King has also discussed the influence of Bram Stoker's bloody vampire saga, *Dracula* (1897), on his own novel. He has taken out the sexual element (because he believes sexual perversion is omnipresent in this country), but King's undead sport all the insignia of the traditional vampire saga: they lust for blood, shun the sun, eschew garlic, and fly away at the sign of the cross.

But King does not have Bram Stoker's faith in science and rationality. He is all too aware of holes in the ozone layer, nerve gas, and the neutron bomb, all products of a science that is far too careless, and so, in his novel, King makes superstition triumph.

Asked how he got the idea in the first place, King said in a 1983 lecture at a Massachusetts library, "Skeletons in the Closet: An Evening at the Billerica Library," that he had been teaching *Dracula* in high school and liking it better every semester. Finally, he asked "the magic question. What would happen if Dracula came back today?"

His wife, Tabitha, suggested, "Well, he'd land at Port Authority in New York and get run over by a taxicab and that'd be the end of him."

But Chris Chesley came up with a different scenario. "But suppose he came back to a little town somewhere

Bela Lugosi (right) as Count Dracula and Helen Chandler as Mina Seward in the 1931 horror movie *Dracula,* based on Bram Stoker's classic 1897 novel. King credits Stoker's book as the inspiration for *'Salem's Lot.* While teaching the novel at Hampden Academy, King pondered, "What would happen if Dracula came back today?"

inland in Maine. You know, you go through some of those little towns and everybody could be dead and you'd never know." Chesley does not even remember the conversation, but it haunted King until he recycled it into 'Salem's Lot. This habit of using people, places, and stories from his life in his fiction is pervasive.

In fact, Eric Norden began his 1983 *Playboy* interview with King with a question that underlines that interaction:

The protagonist of 'Salem's Lot, a struggling young author with a resemblance to his creator, confesses at one point "Sometimes when I'm lying in bed at night, I make up a *Playboy Interview* about me." [Now that it's happening] How does it feel?

"It feels great. I love it!" King answered. In that interview, King places himself in the long and honorable tradition of storytelling that begins with the ancient Greek bards and medieval minnesingers. He sees himself as "the modern equivalent of the old Welsh sin eater, the wandering bard who would be called . . . when somebody was on his deathbed. The family would feed him, because while he was eating, he was also consuming all the sins of the dying person . . . [whose] soul would fly to heaven untarnished, washed clean." Sin eaters died fat, with everyone believing they would drop straight down to hell.

King sees himself and other horror writers as taking upon themselves the task of defusing the "fears and anxieties and insecurities" of their time. He says, "We're sitting in the darkness beyond the flickering warmth of your fire, cackling into our cauldrons and spinning out our spider webs of words, all the time sucking the sickness from your minds and spewing it out into the night."

King wrote in *Danse Macabre,* "I recognize horror as the finest emotion, and so I will try to terrorize the reader. But if I find I cannot terrify him/her, I will try to horrify; and if I find that I cannot horrify, I'll go for the gross-out."

Landscape and places clearly structure King's works. The influence of Nathaniel Hawthorne's primitive forests, claustrophobic villages, and haunted houses, like the Pyncheon mansion in *The House of the Seven Gables* (1851), has often been remarked on. In *Danse Macabre,* King talks of paying homage to Hawthorne. Certainly Hawthorne's Goodman Brown of the short story "Young Goodman Brown" and Arthur Dimmesdale of *The Scarlet Letter* made the kind of journeys that King's characters make a century later. For Hawthorne, however, the individual must establish communion, whereas for King the individual must reject the dominant community's values in order to survive.

In 1976, Brian DePalma directed the film version of *Carrie,* still considered by most critics to be one of the best movie adaptations of a King book. The story is sad, the viewer feels for this strange girl, and the audience comes to understand why she unleashes her horrible anger. The book and the movie both capture the universal lonely, left-out feeling that afflicts so many high school students.

Actress Sissy Spacek, who played Carrie, regarded the character as "a secret poet" and "thought about the terrible feeling of having to suppress one's true nature" as she developed the character. Film critic Donald Peary said, "Spacek is painfully convincing." She "puts us firmly on her side—we identify with her depression, her happiness when invited to the prom, and her need for revenge when the one happy night of her life is ruined by her mother and schoolmate."

Also in 1976, King wrote a guest article for the *New York Times Book Review.* He talked about how a writer like David Madden, whose work he deems excellent, can spend six years writing the admirable novel *Bijou* and

An artist captures the grandiose Pyncheon mansion and its huge elm tree in this illustration from Nathaniel Hawthorne's 1851 novel *The House of the Seven Gables*. King acknowledges Hawthorne's impact on his work; both authors set their stories in New England, writing about a particular kind of people, customs, and traditions that are authentic to the area. King said, "If you're going to live in a place all your life, and if you want to write seriously, you almost have to write about that place."

earn only $15,000 from his work. At the time, King expected to make half a million dollars for eight months' work. Yet he could not feel guilty, because he knew he was writing as honestly as he could.

Nonetheless, King had a difficult and depressing year. He started several novels that did not work out. He shifted from one draft to another, finally focusing on *Firestarter*. The book would not be published until 1980.

In 1977, King moved his family to England with intentions of staying for a year. There he met horror writer Peter Straub, with whom, years later, he would coauthor *The Talisman*. After just three months, the Kings returned to Maine to buy a summer home in Center Lovell.

In the same year, King published *The Shining*, his first hardcover best-seller. This is another solid human drama;

Carrie White, portrayed by actress Sissy Spacek in the 1976 film version of *Carrie,* stands in fury, drenched with pigs' blood, just before she uses her telekinetic powers to cause explosions and fires in the town of Chamberlain, Maine. The movie, directed by Brian DePalma, is considered by most critics to be one of the best adaptations of a King book.

it is really about a family's unraveling. Initially, King liked the scene where the woman gets out of the bathtub and pursues the child, Danny. But he scared himself while doing the rewrite; in many of his televised interviews, he describes the feeling of "oh no, it's the lady in the tub, thirty more pages and I have to face the lady in the tub!"

The Overlook Hotel, like Marsten House of 'Salem's Lot, is a typical haunted house, straight out of traditional Gothic fiction. King pays homage in *The Shining* to Edgar Allan Poe's "Masque of the Red Death." In that terrifying tale, the opulently dressed revelers who have taken refuge in a castle confront death, the plague, which is personified by a figure wearing a black disguise. An even stronger influence on King's novel is Poe's "Fall of the House of Usher." In King's hotel, special rooms, most notably the Colorado Lounge and room 217, act as gateways to alternate worlds and function the way Poe's crypts and chambers do.

Back in Maine, King became politically active again, this time campaigning in a fight against censorship in his home state. Disgusted by the idea of banning books, he has remained involved in this struggle. Though his books are often banned, that is not why he supports the First Amendment (freedom of speech and of the press). He sees censorship as "repulsive to the whole idea of education." He remains dedicated to the right of authors to write and readers to read what they wish. In 1986, he was the Friends of the Library featured speaker for Banned Books Week in Virginia Beach, Virginia.

King began to feel trapped by his fame and his reputation as a horror writer. His publisher, Doubleday, fearful that his public would tire of King if too many of his books came out at the same time, would publish just one King blockbuster each year. Because he often writes two novels per year, as well as short stories, the backlog was considerable. He worried that his early work might easily grow stale.

He went to his editor, Elaine Koster, at New American Library, his paperback publisher, and asked if she would be willing to publish *Getting It On* under a pseudonym. He chose Guy Pillsbury, his maternal grandfather's name.

When people at New American Library connected Pillsbury with King, King rebaptized himself and his novel. In 1977, the same year that *The Shining* came out, New American Library published *Rage,* the revision of *Getting It On,* using the pseudonym Richard Bachman for the first time.

Begun in 1965 when King was 17, *Rage* took seven years to complete. Charlie Decker, a high school student who shoots his algebra teacher and takes over the class, narrates the story. King does here what he will do again and again, culminating in *The Stand:* he isolates a group of people and subjects them to stress. Social structure breaks down, revealing darker, more primitive patterns. The first half of the book went virtually unrevised. Before *Carrie* was accepted, King had submitted *Rage* to Bill Thompson, an editor at Doubleday and an important influence on King. Doubleday came close to publishing it but decided against it. Possibly, King would never have evolved into the master of the horror story had he succeeded in "straight fiction."

Rage was very different from his other novels. King says, "All the Bachman books are sad books. They all have downbeat endings. I don't think the ending of a novel is particularly important, though a lot of people do. I'm more interested in how people react along the way. As far as I'm concerned, we're *all* going to come to an unhappy ending."

The Bachman novels fall easily into the naturalist tradition. The way the naturalists look at the world seems accurate to King. He told one interviewer, "I'm not very

Free-spirited King rides his motorcycle through Maine. His reputation as a renegade writer still exists today—in 1994, King rode his new Harley Davidson to 10 cities across the country to promote his novel *Insomnia*.

optimistic about the world." He is like "all those people of the naturalistic school [who] believed once you pull out one rock, it's sort of a relentless slide into the pit."

Though the condition of society looks insecure and disturbing, King says, "I try to do as well by my family as I can. I try to raise my kids to be good people. You know, the good guys. But I don't think the future looks bright."

Richard Bachman's *Rage* sold moderately well but was not as conspicuous a best-seller as the Stephen King books were. Still, he was relieved to have another outlet. The pressure of being King, the master of horror, was arduous. Though his fans would vehemently disagree, King has said, "I'm not a great artist but I've always felt impelled to write."

Over the coming years, he would publish four more novels under the pseudonym Richard Bachman. New American Library treated Bachman well. Koster kept his identity a secret from some of her own senior executives, despite the enormous pressures to tell the world that Bachman was really King. Grateful to New American Library for the way they treated "my friend Bachman," King decided to work exclusively with that publisher.

6 "Spider Webs of Words"

IN 1978, KING BRIEFLY RETURNED TO TEACHING as a writer-in-residence at his alma mater, the University of Maine at Orono. The King family rented a house that fronted a busy road in Orrington, near Bangor. The neighborhood children had constructed a little graveyard in the woods for the many animals killed by trucks on the highway. Among the victims was King's daughter Naomi's cat, Smucky. Tabitha convinced her husband that they had to tell Naomi about the fate of her pet, and upon hearing the bad news, Naomi cried and cried.

Three days after Smucky's funeral, the idea for the novel *Pet Sematary* came to King. His younger son, Owen, had been running toward the road when King caught hold of him. What if not only the cat but also the two-year-old son were killed? That night King dreamed of "a corpse walking up and down outside the house," he told writer and critic Douglas E. Winter. King thought about funeral customs, a subject that he had preferred to avoid until now. He knew that he would write a novel that would consciously retell that most depressing of short stories, W. W. Jacobs's "The Monkey's Paw" (1902). In

King imitates the mounted head of a rattlesnake he is holding. Nearly all of his novels have become best-sellers, making King one of the most successful authors in the world.

that tale, grieving parents are granted their most fervent wish: to have their son come back from the dead. Their son returns to them, but he is merely a powdery corpse. The moral: do not wish for what you cannot have.

Stephen King published *Pet Sematary* in 1983. He had completed the first draft in 1979, but because the book dealt with the realistic death of a child, King believed it was too horrible to read and hesitated having it published. However, to fulfill a contract with Doubleday, he agreed to publish the book.

King found writing *Pet Sematary* "a gloomy exercise, like an endless marathon run." Images from the book—the dead child, the funeral home, and the mortician's room—were always with him, even when he was trying to teach. One of his own worst fears has always been that something would happen to one of his children. His early fears for his youngest child irrationally resurfaced, as the boy once had been misdiagnosed as a hydrocephalic, one who has a congenital condition in which water accumulates around the brain, enlarging the skull and squeezing the brain.

Whenever an innocent child dies in one of his works, as Tad Trenton does in *Cujo,* King suffers. In *Pet Sematary,* not only did he write about the death of a child, one subject that he never wanted to address, but he had to deal with the aftermath: "the funeral parlors, the burial, the grief, and . . . the guilt—the feeling that you are somehow at fault. . . . It was like looking through a window into something that could be."

Tabitha King cried when she read the story. The novel was so painful that King stuck the first draft into a drawer, and when a television interviewer asked whether King had ever written anything too horrible to be printed, he referred to the buried manuscript, stirring up rumors among his millions of fans of a book more horrifying than any they had already experienced.

The fact that *Pet Sematary* did appear at all might be the happy result of an unfortunate contract dispute with Doubleday. To get a substantial amount of money that was due him, King had to offer them a novel. He rewrote the first draft in 1982, and one year later when the book was published, for the publicity campaign, he gave Doubleday permission to use the previous rumors that had been stirred up. But King himself took no part in promoting the book, nor would he talk about it until his January 15, 1984, interview with Douglas E. Winter. King said,

A set from the 1989 movie *Pet Sematary,* which was based on King's novel, shows the cemetery for pets. The idea for the book came from a real pet graveyard in Orrington, Maine, that the neighborhood children created. The "Pets Sematary" (a child's misspelling) had become the resting place for King's daughter's cat, Smucky.

> [The book] never left my mind, it never ceased to trouble me. I was trying to teach school, and the boy was always there, the mortician's room was always there. . . . So it hurts me to talk about it, it hurts me to think about it. *Pet Sematary* is the one book I haven't reread—I never want to go there again, because it is a real cemetary.

In the writing workshops King ran that year at the university, he taught his students the way he thought writers needed to be treated. For example, he made sure his writing workshops had a friendly atmosphere, and he took the young writers seriously. But, King told Paul Janeczko in a February 1980 interview published in *English Journal,* which is intended for English teachers, creativity cannot be taught. Teachers are useful, however, once writers have developed to a certain point. These talented novices can be taught to write better. They can learn to experiment with point of view, to pace the work, to spot their themes, and to rewrite to integrate beginnings into the endings.

He found that teaching creative writing had been easier in high school, where students had selected the course just to have fun. King felt he could say, "'Rip this out and put it here.' And they did it. They took a lot more chances."

In college, where egos are "mortally involved," he became timid, fearful of destroying students' confidence. "Unfortunately, with a lot of poetry students you're laboring under a lot of terrible burdens like [poet] Rod McKuen and ["Star Trek" actor] Leonard Nimoy and Hallmark greeting cards. You've got to work against that." Young poets are far too easily influenced by phony sentimentality and pseudoscientific solutions.

He assigned a few novels, including James Cain's *Double Indemnity* and David Morrell's *First Blood.* He says, "If a writer isn't reading, he's in big trouble anyway." From what they read, writers learn what to do and what not to do. Students need to get to the point when they can say, "I do better stuff than that."

But King is quick to point out that writers need to be talented in the first place for all the hard work to pay off. He uses himself as an example. He has played guitar since he was 16 years old but says, "I've not progressed much beyond where I was at sixteen, playing 'Louie, Louie' and 'Little Deuce Coupe' on rhythm guitar with a group called the MoonSpinners." He still plays now and then, especially to cheer himself up when he gets the blues. But he says, "I think Eric Clapton is still safe."

The talented writers have to work to refine that talent. "Refining talent," King says, "is merely a matter of exercise. If you work out with weights for fifteen minutes a day over a course of ten years, you're gonna get muscles.

If you write for an hour and a half a day for ten years, you're gonna turn into a good writer."

While King was a writer-in-residence at the University of Maine, he developed and began to write *Danse Macabre,* which was published in 1981. It is an analysis of the horror genre in literature, film, and television. The idea for the book came from his friend and first editor, Bill Thompson, and grew out of the course that he was teaching. He included notes about his own evolution and that of the radio shows, the movies, the comic books, and the sociopolitical conditions that surface in his work, and he discusses what the horror genre does.

The horror story lets readers prove that they are not afraid of the monstrous and that, however unpleasant,

In 1981, King autographs *Danse Macabre,* his non-fiction analysis of the horror genre. His wife, Tabitha, was also on hand to sign copies of her first novel, *Small World,* at a Bangor, Maine, bookstore.

the real world is better than what is on the page or the screen. It confirms the status quo. In *Danse Macabre,* which King calls his "dance with death," he asserts that horror "appeals to the conservative Republican in a three-piece suit who resides within all of us; its main purpose is to reaffirm the virtues of the norm by showing us what awful things happen to people who venture into taboo lands."

He finds "a strong moral code" in most horror tales. Apologizing for the academic metaphor, he suggests "that the horror tale details the outbreak of some Dionysian [frenzied] madness in an Apollonian [rational] existence, and that horror will continue until the Dionysian forces have been repelled and the Apollonian norm restored again."

He says, "We fear the Ghost for much the same reason as we fear the Werewolf: it is the deep part of us that need not be bound by piffling Apollonian restrictions. It can walk through walls, disappear, speak in the voices of strangers. It is the Dionysian part of us . . . but it is still us."

In horror stories, as in fairy tales, readers become part of larger forces, counters in the battle of humans against the dark powers of the irrational and the supernatural; and most important, they explore the "only truly universal rite of passage": death.

Stephen King immerses himself in this world of horror by doing at least a two-hour stint of writing every day—that is, six pages, or 1,250 words per day. He also reads every day, sometimes rereading his own novels. He prefers fiction to nonfiction, which he finds too scary. He has learned about pace and plot from competent authors like John D. MacDonald and Ed McBain, who entertain as they teach. He has learned "what not to do" from the works of authors like Jacqueline Susann and Harold Robbins, "where characters seem cardboard."

Characters should be real, able to move on their own. What they do in the course of the story must not violate their nature. King insists that readers have to care about the people, which means they must behave realistically, not just move to fit the plot an author has constructed. "They must have thickness," he says. "You don't get scared of monsters; you get scared for people."

In 1978, he published *Night Shift,* a collection of short stories written during his destitute days in college and after graduation. They stand up so well today that it is hard to believe the pressure he was under when he wrote them. Nineteen seventy-eight was an exceptionally good year for King because in addition to the success of *Night Shift,* it was the year that he published *The Stand.*

In the mid-seventies, King had read about an accidental spill of a chemical-biological weapon in Utah that killed herds of sheep. The toxic substance might have wiped out an equal number of people had the wind blown in the other direction. By chance, he heard a "preacher dilating upon the text, 'Once in every generation the plague will fall among them.'" He posted those words above his desk, put them together with the gas shortages, Watergate, President Nixon's resignation, the toxic spill in Utah, another technological disaster, and he began the work that would weigh more than 12 pounds by the time he had finished it.

At times he hated *The Stand,* but King always felt "compelled to go on with it. There was a crazy, joyful feeling about the book. I couldn't wait to sit down in front of the typewriter every morning and slip back into that world where Randy Flagg could sometimes become a crow, sometimes a wolf, and where the big battle was not for gasoline allocations but for human souls. . . . I was doing a fast, happy tapdance on the grave of the whole world."

King poses with the mask of the evil character Randall Flagg of *The Stand*. The novel, a favorite of King fans and originally published in 1978, was made into a television miniseries in 1994. The mask today is a part of the movie memorabilia collection of New York's Planet Hollywood restaurant.

The story of a plague set loose by the military that threatens to destroy all life on earth came out of a time when the Arabs suddenly shut off the supply of oil. Long lines formed at the gas pumps. Fistfights broke out. Prices soared, and people installed locks on their tanks to keep thieves from siphoning off the little gas they had.

King wrote about *The Stand* that "an Apollonian society is disrupted by a Dionysian force . . . a deadly strain of superflu." The novel is about the battle of two groups of survivors, the Apollonian and the Dionysian. The Apollonians incorporate rational, orderly creative principles, whereas the Dionysians exemplify frenzied, intuitive revelers. In the end, a reformulated Apollonian community celebrates its continuing existence with the birth of a healthy daughter. In the best of King, love and loyalty to a small group of worthy individuals serves a redemptive function.

The plague is called "Captain Trips," which is the nickname of the rock star Jerry Garcia of the Grateful Dead, whose music and lyrics suggest drug-induced experiences. The critic Joseph Reino notes "allegorical dimensions. For as drug junkets go 'tripping' across the United States (hypodermically from youth to youth), so the fatal disease goes 'tripping' from person to person."

Even with 400 pages deleted, the first version of *The Stand* was 800 pages long. The uncut version, 1,200 pages long, was published in 1990. The reader observes Mother Abigail, an ancient black woman who practices white magic (magic that is used to fight evil), and her followers, who wander into the woods, shunning autos, weapons, and modern machinery. Their instincts and courage triumph over the evil Flagg, the wizard of technology, and his disciples, "who sacrifice moral responsibility in favor of a commitment to technology," demonstrating what is, according to Tony Magistrale, one of Stephen King's most important concerns.

In 1979, King published *The Dead Zone,* the first of his novels to hit number one on the *New York Times* best-seller list. The wheel of fortune is the book's central symbol; Johnny Smith, an everyman, its protagonist; and the nature of political and personal chaos its subject matter.

Smith can see into the future, where he perceives that Greg Stillson, as president, will go mad and provoke a nuclear holocaust. Smith must act to support his society, which he does by exposing the villains: one, the Castle Rock rapist, who appears to be a trusted deputy sheriff; the other, the tainted politician Stillson, whom he attempts to assassinate.

Also in 1979, as Richard Bachman, King published *The Long Walk,* which he had completed in 1967, when he was a freshman at the University of Maine, and stored away in a trunk with other unpublished material. He did not have a car when he started the book, so he put in a lot of time hitchhiking wherever he needed to go. As usual, King made good use of his experience.

The novel follows a dozen or so of the 100 14- to 16-year-olds who march all the way through Maine. Any marcher whose pace drops below four miles per hour is shot by soldiers not much older than the marchers themselves. The sole survivor gets one wish as his reward. King conjures up the specter of the ancient Roman gladiators and their barbaric games as well as that of contemporary sports figures who use steroids to enhance their performance.

Over the years, a phony biography of Bachman evolved. The imaginary author had been born in New York in 1947. He had joined the merchant marine after high school. Then he had settled in New Hampshire, writing and running a dairy farm. To explain his isolation, Bachman was burdened with a face deformed by cancer, a sick wife, and the loss of his only child, who drowned at age six.

But Bachman's connections to King abound. At the Library of Congress, King or his agent are listed on the copyright forms, and the Bachman books are dedicated to people King knew, such as college professors Jim Bishop, Burton Hatlen, and Ted Holmes, and a fellow Hampden Academy teacher, Charlotte Littlefield. The last book, however, is dedicated to Bachman's long-suffering wife, Claudia. Furthermore, all the Bachman books have Maine settings and often make use of places that appear in King's stories.

On television, a well-made, hair-raising miniseries version of *'Salem's Lot* was shown in November 1979.

James Mason portrayed the sinister antiques dealer, and Reggie Nalder played the vampire. Critics found them terrifying. David Soul played the successful writer who returns to his hometown to find vampires.

In 1980, the Kings bought the William Arnold House, an old Victorian mansion on West Broadway built between 1854 and 1856, the only Italianate villa in Bangor. By fate or by chance, the red house with towers was the same one that the young Tabitha had dreamed of living in when she had walked up West Broadway with a friend years before. The Kings hired craftsmen from Center Lovell to modernize the interior of the house and the barn, which became the hub of their activities. The renovations took years to complete.

King stands outside his Victorian mansion in Bangor. After moving around often, the Kings bought the 23-room house in 1980 to use as their permanent winter residence. The family personalized the house by making office space for both Stephen and Tabitha, and by installing stained glass bat windows and building a wrought-iron fence with bats and spiderwebs to enclose the property.

Located in the historic district of Bangor, the house looks much the same as it did originally, but spiffier. To the exterior the Kings added a beautiful, intricate wrought-iron fence. The aptly named Terry Steel, a member of the Artist Blacksmith Association of North America, designed and crafted the "270 lineal feet of hand forged fence, weighing 11,000 pounds, punctuated by two gates composed of spiders, webs, goat heads, and winged bats." King, a fan of Batman, wanted the bats. Tabitha asked for spiders and their webs.

Inside the house is the original golden oak entry and mahogany woodwork, plus a modern kitchen, including a counter high enough for the six-foot-four-inch King to knead bread. The bread is set to rise in a nearby warming oven made of bricks from Royal River, near the town where King grew up.

Located in the square tower is "a large orange telescope," which King, "an amateur astronomer, moves out onto the front lawn on clear nights." Tabitha's office—designed for Stephen, who found it too noisy—is situated in the cylindrical tower.

The barn has been completely renovated to provide family living space; King's office is located above that, complete with a stained-glass bat window. The office also has a secret entrance—through a thick door that masquerades as a bookcase when closed, and up a narrow staircase. On the shelves that line the walls of the well-lit office are copies of all his works, including foreign language editions.

In the seating area of the office, framed jigsaw puzzles of actors Marilyn Monroe and Humphrey Bogart, as well as a New Hampshire license plate that reads "Cujo," hang on the wall. King's bathroom accommodates a black Jacuzzi and black sink.

Tabitha can find flaws in the kitchen, which the Kings carved out of six rooms, though it has a red sink, a dumbwaiter to take clothes to the new second-story laundry room, white cabinets trimmed with oak, and butcher-block counters. But the magnificent indoor pool she finds perfect. Tabitha, who did not learn to swim until she was 30, now swims every day. The house is amazing, complete with secret passageways and a ghost, who Tabitha feels must be the reason that the large, elegant living room is a rather "cold room."

Maine is not only the state where King was born; it is also the place where he has chosen to live. When people ask him why, he says that he is a hick at heart and Maine is where he feels at home, or that Bangor has no distractions, or that his children do not need to be celebrities there. They can go to public school. Tabitha can write, and so can he. In 1986, he described his routine in an interview with Elaine Landa for *Inside,* the newspaper of Orono High School, in Orono, Maine.

He writes in the mornings, eats lunch with Tabitha, reads or does interviews, and when the kids were still living at home, he made breakfast for them before he took his four-mile walk, and "hung out" with them after work.

In 1980, King published *Firestarter,* a novel about a little girl, Charlie McGee, who starts fires with telekinetic powers. She must flee from members of a cruel and incompetent government organization, the Shop, who fed her parents a hallucinogenic drug, Lot Six, the source of the terrifying power she inherited from her mother, who died. She even has the ability to start fires while asleep. The Shop wants Charlie dead because she has the "power to someday crack the very planet in two."

Critic Joseph Reino feels that King has produced more than a horror novel. It is "a pitiless ethics of a bleak and sexually grotesque America." In the end, Charlie McGee survives, her powers as Firestarter intact, which leaves the reader to deal with the possibility that without meaning to do harm, Charlie might, nonetheless, precipitate an

Stephen King types away in his home office. He writes for at least two hours each day, composing about six pages, or 1,250 words per day. Sometimes the story flows easier than at other times; for example, when King was writing *The Stand,* he was anxious to get started every morning. He said, "I was doing a fast, happy tapdance on the grave of the whole world."

apocalypse because she cannot always control her pyro-technic capabilities.

Also in 1980, Stanley Kubrick directed a terrifying movie version of *The Shining,* starring Jack Nicholson as Jack Torrance. Although the movie received good reviews, King was disappointed with the film. He feels that the movie, "a shock-a-minute terrorfest," misses much of the point of the book, which is really about the unraveling and breakdown of a family.

In 1981, Tabitha published a short story, "The Blue Chair," and her first novel, *Small World.* Though she also sets her stories in Maine, she has a gentler approach to storytelling, focusing on the passions and moral choices of people who live and work in small towns. She does not write horror. Nor does she write blockbusters, but reviewers applaud her works for their comic flair, feisty heroines, and accurate sense of place.

Using his own fears as inspiration, in 1981 King published *Cujo,* arguably his bleakest novel. He describes the process of writing a book that incorporates one of his own greatest fears: the idea that one of his children will die. In *Cujo,* a huge, rabid dog traps a woman in a car with her sick child, who, in the end, dies. That literary death upset King; he had not planned on having a child die, but the book seemed to write itself, and it was the only way the story could end.

Among the awards he won in 1981 are the Career Alumni Award from the University of Maine and the World Fantasy Award for best short fiction from the World Fantasy Association, which met in Providence, Rhode Island, that year. In "Do the Dead Sing?", also known as "The Reach," a most appealing tale and one of King's personal favorites, Stella Flanders, a 95-year-old who is dying of cancer, walks Goat Island, Maine, for the first time. Her walk, an archetypal journey over the frozen Reach, takes her into her past. She sees those who have died standing hand in hand before her, singing hymns.

And King's alter ego published the best of Richard Bachman's novels, *Roadwork,* written in 1974, just after King had completed *'Salem's Lot.* Bachman novels have nothing of the supernatural about them; rather, they are psychological. Here, the protagonist, Bart Dawes, tries to make sense of the death by cancer of his beloved child. He fails to make crucial decisions in his own life, losing his wife and business as a result. Finally, he makes a seemingly mad stand against the road that will replace his home, in the mistaken hope that his actions will make people think about the damage uninformed technological changes can do.

In 1982, sometime around Halloween, King bought an AM radio station as an investment, realizing a potent childhood fantasy, to keep his beloved hard rock music on the airwaves. The call letters WACZ, inherited from the Acton Corporation, were changed to WZON in homage to "The Twilight Zone" and King's book *The Dead Zone.* The phrase, "You're in the rock zone," identified the connection: King, horror, and rock and roll.

King began to use a word processor to write, producing almost immediately the short story "Word Processor of the Gods," published by *Playboy* in January 1983, reprinted in *Skeleton Crew,* and adapted for the television

King reads *Creepshow,* his compilation of five unrelated horror stories, which was published in 1982. A tribute to the E. C. horror comics of the 1950s, the book consisted of 424 individual comic strip panels drawn by Berni Wrightson.

series "Tales from the Darkside." The story makes wonderful use of the computer's delete function, which lets writers effortlessly and endlessly replace old versions with new. Richard Hagstrom erases his fat, sodden wife and dull son and replaces them with the dead wife and dead diligent son of his drunken brother. "Word Processor of the Gods" not only makes use of current events but plays with the thematic material of *Pet Sematary* and W. W. Jacobs's "The Monkey's Paw." But in this version an author gets away with the raising of the dead.

In 1982, King published *Different Seasons,* a collection of short stories, *Creepshow,* and a limited edition of *The Dark Tower: The Gunslinger.* King also brought out another Richard Bachman novel, *The Running Man,* which was written during one frenetic weekend in 1971. Describing a barbaric sporting event set in the future, the novel was another dark look at American sports and its spectators, who resemble bloodthirsty mobs, betting madly on contests of savage violence. *The Running Man* is the least adroit of the Bachman books according to critics.

In October 1982, King appeared in the movie *Creepshow,* based on his book. King said the idea of the film was "simply to put people in movie theaters and see if we can scare the hell out of them. I want people crawling under the seats with popcorn and jujubes in their hair."

The book *Creepshow* was his homage to the E. C. Comics of the 1950s, a series of horror comics driven out of business by the special Senate committee whose chairman was Senator Joseph McCarthy. McCarthy's committee accused E. C. Comics of polluting children's minds. Caught reading a *Creepshow* comic, a young boy is sent to bed by his disapproving father, who throws the comic into the trash. Wind lifts the pages and the five episodes of the movie unfold. In the movie, King plays a

King makes his acting debut in "The Lonesome Death of Jordy Verrill," a segment of *Creepshow*, which was based on his original screenplay. King said the idea of the movie is "simply to put people in movie theaters and see if we can scare the hell out of them. I want people crawling under the seats with popcorn and jujubes in their hair."

dim-witted country bumpkin who has a close encounter with a meteorite. King's son Joe, who was eight or nine years old at the time, also appears in the film.

Joe had a good time, according to his father, particularly one evening after a late shoot when the family stopped at McDonald's for dinner. Joe, dressed in pajamas for his movie role, still wore makeup—a realistic bruise on his face, supposedly planted there by his character's father. King reports, "By the time we left, about fifteen minutes later, everyone had been outside to see the kid in his pajamas with this great big bruise on the side of his face."

In the summer of 1982, King was guest of honor, or roastee, at the NECON (NorthEastern Regional Fantasy Convention), held at Roger Williams College in Bristol, Rhode Island. And for Christmas, by way of greetings, King began to send his friends episodes of a self-published comic horror novel, *The Plant.* The story includes a seedy editor of paperback books as the protagonist.

In 1983, Tabitha published her second book, *Caretakers.* King published *Christine, Cycle of the Werewolf,* and *Pet Sematary.* In the prologue to *Christine,* King calls the book "a lover's triangle," involving a boy, a car, and a woman. Christine is a 20-year-old mankiller "with terrific headlights, a sleek body, . . . built for speed." Certainly, the novel can be read as an attack on America's love affair with technology, especially the automobile, America's dream machine. Christine, a 1958 Plymouth Fury, turns into a monster that no longer has any need of the human beings who created her, because Christine can even repair herself. Reason produces machines, but as critic Tony Magistrale points out, reason is "displaced by irrational and malevolent forces."

In King's work, whenever creators abdicate responsibility for what they have made, supernatural demons take over. When the protagonist of *Christine,* Arnie, isolates himself from the human community, he cuts himself off from family and the chance for mature love. His jealous mistress, the machine, enslaves him.

Like Mary Shelley's character Dr. Frankenstein, King's Arnie wants to bring life to inanimate matter. As Magistrale points out, neither Frankenstein nor Arnie will destroy the monster he sets loose on the world, and both perish. "An implicit warning exists in both books: the more sophisticated our technological expertise, the greater the potential of losing control over it." Christine may return.

King has explored the theme of malevolent machines in a number of stories. Among them are "The Mangler," "Uncle Otto's Truck," and "Trucks," collected in *Night Shift*. "Trucks" was made into a movie, *Maximum Overdrive*, directed by King himself in 1986. Later, in *The Tommyknockers*, published in 1987, King deals with a society that he fears has let technology run mad, a recurrent theme in his work.

While rewriting *Christine*, King actually scared himself. Once again his own story surprised him. King never expected "the kid to run people down," he told an audience at a lecture on "Banned Books and Other Concerns" in Virginia Beach, Virginia, in 1986. He found facing it all over again as he went through the manuscript quite disturbing.

"Sometimes [stories] get out of control and they are like the car itself; they start to run by themselves and they don't always turn out the way you think they are going to turn out," he said. The same thing happened with *Cujo*. King did not expect the little boy trapped in a broken-down Pinto with his mother to die, but he did, and readers wrote to complain.

In response, King wrote, "I don't know. . . . I was working away . . . and the kid just croaked. I couldn't help it." He added, "The fact is, that's the moral ending—cause kids don't always live—sometimes kids do die."

However, in the movie version of *Cujo*, to please his audience who he feared might lynch him, King let little Tad Trenton live. He points out, however, that a worse fate awaits the child: Tad Trenton, after all, has been bitten by a rabid 200-pound Saint Bernard and will die a horrible death.

Nineteen eighty-three was a banner year for King movies: *The Dead Zone, Cujo,* and *Christine* were all released. King paid $15,000 out of his own pocket in royalties for the lyrics to the rock-and-roll music used in the movie version of *Christine,* which opened in December. The movies did well at the box office, but the usual snobbery about them still surfaced. Many critics dismissed them as more of that Stephen King gross-out horror.

In 1983, when Stephanie Spruce Leonard, Tabitha's sister and Stephen's secretary, took maternity leave, Shirley Sonderegger joined King's office staff. He was getting close to 500 pieces of mail per week, most of which needed some sort of reply. Today, Sonderegger deals with business arrangements for Tabitha and Stephen, and she continues to handle all inquiries about King's work.

King pets "Cujo" at a public appearance in Truth or Consequences, New Mexico. The 1981 novel *Cujo,* about a rabid Saint Bernard, was one of three King books that was made into a movie in 1983.

In June 1983, at a new height of popularity, Stephen King earned the supreme accolade, an interview with *Playboy* magazine. King revealed what most people already seemed to know about him: that he is a regular guy blessed with an active imagination, a strong sense of community responsibility, and a deep commitment to his wife, children, and work.

7 ★ A Vacation in Castle Rock

I N 1984, STEPHEN KING RESPONDED to one of his most important critics—his 13-year-old daughter, Naomi, who avoided reading horror novels, even those written by her father. It bothered him that she did not like to read his books. Hoping to interest her in one of his stories, he wrote *The Eyes of the Dragon*, a dark fairy tale. King's yarn about the handsome Prince Peter and the evil Flagg was different from anything else he had written. He dedicated it to Naomi and to his friend Peter Straub's son, Ben, both of whom appear in the novel, teaming up to help Prince Peter—falsely accused of murdering the king, his father—escape from the tower in which he has been imprisoned.

Naomi read *The Eyes of the Dragon* and liked it. King said that Naomi had paid him the highest compliment. To her, the only thing wrong with the adult fairy tale was that it ended. He published the book himself in a limited edition through his own Philtrum Press, established in 1982, holding a lottery to decide which fans would be able to buy the $127 first edition. Viking published the hardcover edition in 1987.

Stephen King sits in a Beverly Hills, California, hotel room in 1986. The 1980s saw King explore the movie industry—behind the scenes as a director and screenwriter and on-screen as an actor.

King and Kenneth Linkous (right) hold up artwork for *The Eyes of the Dragon.* Linkous illustrated the story that King wrote for and dedicated to his daughter, Naomi, who disliked reading horror novels. A lottery was held to buy the limited edition adult fairy tale, which was printed by King's own Philtrum Press in 1984. Three years later, Viking published a trade edition of the book.

In 1984, he also published *The Talisman,* which he wrote with Peter Straub, who, when he first read King's work, felt as if he had suddenly discovered a long-lost brother because they had similar goals.

The two writers felt strong affinities to each other's works though their styles are diametrically opposed. Critic Douglas E. Winter calls Peter Straub a stylist whose fiction is "structurally complex," the "aesthetic conscience of the modern horror field." He says Stephen King writes intuitively and prides himself on a "colloquial storyteller's prose" that is accessible to just about anyone.

They had had the idea of collaborating on a book when they first met in London, England, during King's three-month sojourn there. In 1980, Straub came to the United States, and the two developed the story line. They wrote alternate sections, trying each other's style and voice, Straub's "good prose" and King's "plain" style (King calls it his "Big Mac and a large fries" way of writing).

They also read a number of epics, such as Dante's *Divine Comedy* and Tolkien's *Lord of the Rings,* and books about epic heroes by scholars like Joseph Campbell. Their novel, however, is essentially about family. The plot involves a quest: a 12-year-old boy wants to help his dying mother in her battle with cancer, and along the way he discovers truths about the deaths of a father, an uncle, and a twin brother who died as an infant.

The protagonist is named Sawyer, and the book ends with a quotation from Mark Twain's *Tom Sawyer:* "It being strictly a history of a *boy*, it must stop here; the story could not go much further without becoming the history of a man."

Just as Twain's Huckleberry Finn made a symbolic voyage by raft down the Mississippi, young Jack Sawyer makes an archetypal journey west through a violent contemporary America.

Much as Twain criticized his society, King incorporates an attack on what he calls "Reagan's America." His young hero, traveling through a landscape that is polluted both physically and morally, encounters "the ebb and flow of an underclass, the dregs of society, the unhomed and the homeless drifting just below everybody's sight." He learns to value life, and about the damaging effects of "society's dehumanizing power over the individual."

His journey is an education. Sawyer learns about love and friendship. He fits Joseph Campbell's definition of hero, one who benefits not only himself but also his family and society; he seeks power not for himself but in order to save his mother and Mother Earth. *The Talisman* ends with Jack's triumph over the forces of darkness and despair, a traditional ending to an epic.

Though he admits the influence of the psychologist Sigmund Freud on his work, King considers himself more of a Jungian, plumbing the depths of what Carl Jung called the "collective unconscious" to find patterns for his writing. An archetype is a pattern—a universal character, action, or image embedded deep within every human being that occurs in all countries and periods.

Both King and Straub found working together enriching. Straub called it "a wonderful and profound experience, something very few writers ever get the chance to have."

In 1984, New American Library published a hardcover edition of the book that would terminate King's pseudonymous career: *Thinner,* the fifth Richard Bachman novel. Written in 1982, *Thinner* was quintessential King and the beginning of the end of Bachman. It was accompanied by a high-powered publicity campaign that included a photograph of Bachman on the book jacket— the photo was actually that of a total stranger to King, a friend of King's agent. Up until then, Bachman fans who had wanted to meet the author had fallen for a fake biography. They believed that the pathetic man was a one-eyed chicken farmer, made timid by grotesque scars resulting from his bout with cancer.

This time, a clever reader, law student Steve Brown, recognized King's prose style. Brown researched the copyrights of the Bachman books at the Library of Congress and found that Kirby McCauley, King's agent, held four of the copyrights. King himself held the fifth. Brown wrote to King, who phoned Brown, and they talked. Then Brown wrote an article in the *Washington Post*— "The Life and Death of Richard Bachman: Stephen King's Doppelganger." In February 1985, King told the world in the *Bangor Daily News*: Bachman Is King!

In discussing *Thinner,* King told Brown that he was not pleased when his doctor told him that he weighed too much and smoked too many cigarettes. King recalled to Brown that the doctor said, "You've entered heart attack country," a line King uses in the novel. He said he "spent a very angry weekend." He thought about how awful "they were to make me do all these terrible things to save my life." Then he followed his doctor's advice and cut out smoking and lost weight. He discovered, however, that he "didn't want to lose it," and then he asked himself the question that became the core of the novel: "what would happen if somebody started to lose weight and couldn't stop?"

In *Thinner,* an overweight lawyer named William Halleck is cursed by the husband of a gypsy woman whom he had unintentionally killed. In the courtroom where Halleck has just evaded the responsibility for killing the woman in a traffic accident, the husband points a finger at Halleck and says just one word—"thinner." Halleck begins to lose weight and gets thinner and thinner. His predicament raises questions about the potent American maxim, "There's no such thing as too rich or too thin." Comparatively humorous, the novel is quite entertaining, although the character Halleck is not amused by his fate.

Because King always looks at moral issues, *Thinner* became, he said, "a book about responsibilities. If you avoid your obligations, then you always end up hurting your loved ones."

But "humor crept in after a while," King said. "[I] remembered all the things I did when I weighed a lot. I had a paranoid conviction that the scales weighed heavy, no matter what." He would weigh himself only in the

Standing in front of King's Bangor home before the May 1984 premiere of *Firestarter* are (left to right) producer Dino De Laurentiis, actress Drew Barrymore, executive director John Supranovich, and King. The plot of the movie involves a little girl who can start fires with her telekinetic powers.

morning, without clothes, and got furious at the doctor for not letting him go to the bathroom before he got on the scale.

Two more King movies came out in 1984: *Children of the Corn,* which film critic Leonard Maltin calls a "pretty tacky, laughable adaptation" of a King short story, and *Firestarter,* starring Drew Barrymore, which was marginally more successful. In 1985, *Cat's Eye,* a movie adaptation of some of his short stories, was called "heavy handed" and "short on irony, long on mean-spiritedness."

In 1985, New American Library published a compilation of all the Bachman novels called *The Bachman Books.* Now that people knew who Bachman was, there was great interest in the compilation.

Skeleton Crew, another collection of short stories, came out the same year. In addition, with illustrator Berni Wrightson, King contributed a segment to the comic book *Heroes for Hope,* the proceeds of which were donated to famine relief in Africa.

King also became involved with a revival of the old "Twilight Zone" television show. The new TV series, "The New Twilight Zone," was broadcast on CBS. Two of King's stories, "The Word Processor of the Gods" and "Gramma," were adapted for the series. In "Gramma," King makes use of his own struggle in dealing with the death of his grandmother. The central character, Georgie, is home alone with his invalid grandmother, who happens to be a witch, when she dies. The episode, broadcast in February 1986 and scripted by Harlan Ellison, was, according to one critic, "a spooky, atmospheric adaptation of one of Stephen King's most frightening stories."

Castle Rock: The Stephen King Newsletter appeared in January 1985. Edited by Stephanie Leonard, Tabitha's sister, the newsletter seemed a creative way to handle the flood of fan mail that arrived, week after week. A card file

When King became a best-selling novelist, *Castle Rock: The Stephen King Newsletter* was established to help control the flood of fan mail that he received. The newsletter was a way to provide fans with answers to the most commonly asked questions about their favorite writer, who remained uneasy about having such a publication dedicated to himself.

of the thousands of fans who have requested posters or sent copies of his books to be autographed covers one whole wall of King's office. Leonard used to answer each letter, but finally, though King disliked doing it, she had to use a form letter because the volume of correspondence became overwhelming. Less than 1 percent of the letters, King estimates, comes from the lunatic fringe. Often the letter writers offer constructive comments.

Because fans frequently ask the same questions over and over, King, who was appalled by the idea of a Stephen King fan club, sanctioned the newsletter, but only if he did not have to be involved with it. Other members of Tabitha's family helped edit and publish the newsletter.

Stephanie Leonard described her typical workday in an interview with Stephen J. Spignesi, author of *The Shape Under the Sheet: The Complete Stephen King Encyclopedia*, a handy reference work published in 1991.

Leonard explained that she handled business mail and fan mail, manuscripts—editing, research, word processing—travel arrangements, and whatever else needed to be done on a particular day.

She described her years with King as "fast and furious! One day I was sixteen and baby sitting for them when they could scrape up enough money to go to a movie, and the next day I was baby sitting for them while they went to Cannes [France]! My children are just beginning to realize that 'Uncle Steve' is famous."

During the years Stephanie Leonard edited the newsletter, she worked on it almost every day. Occasionally, it printed original stories that had not yet appeared elsewhere. News of King's work, analyses, reviews, satires, puzzles, and a number of "Lists That Matter" were all included in the newsletter. In issue number 7, King picked his 10 favorite movies, among them *Casablanca* (1942), *E. T.* (1982), *Stagecoach* (1939), and *The Wizard of Oz* (1939). Among his least favorite were *Blood Feast* (1979), *Old Yeller* (1957), and his own *Children of the Corn* (1984).

The March 1985 issue of the *Castle Rock* newsletter announced the Bachman-King connection. The November issue included a poll of readers, the majority of whom picked *The Stand* as their favorite King novel.

The first issue of 1986 included an eerie short story by Tabitha King and raised the price of each issue 25 cents to $1.25. The February issue listed King's "High School Horrors," including "The Thing That Wouldn't Shut Up" and "The Smell from Hell." In May, King's daughter, Naomi, reported on a Mohonk Mountain House mystery weekend in New Paltz, New York, with writers Peter Straub, Gahan Wilson, and Donald Westlake. And in the July issue, brother-in-law Christopher Spruce documented King's successful campaign to defeat the Maine Censorship Referendum.

In 1988, Leonard turned *Castle Rock* over to her brother, Spruce. The project was becoming too time-consuming, the subscriber base had shrunk from 5,000 to 1,500, and according to Spruce, King had never "been entirely comfortable with the idea of a newsletter devoted to [him]." The newsletter suspended publication in 1989.

In 1986, King published *It,* a 1,138-page novel, featured as a main selection by the Book of the Month Club, that pulls together all the most frightening bogeymen of childhood into one great beast. The book was also made into a television miniseries, starring Tim Curry as an evil clown.

There are intriguing parallels between *It* and the novella "The Body." In both, innocent young boys make a voyage, confront death, and return wiser and stronger. King indicts the adults of the fictional towns of Castle Rock, the setting of "The Body," and Derry, Maine, the setting of *It* and a center of evil. In the Lloyd H. Elliott lecture he delivered at the University of Maine at Orono on November 6, 1986, King cited William Carlos Williams's epic poem *Paterson,* calling *It* "an epic poem

King sits atop one of the evil machines that comes to life in *Maximum Overdrive,* a 1986 movie based on his short story "Trucks." King made his directorial debut with this film. "I didn't care for [directing] at all," he said later. "I had to work. I wasn't used to working. I hadn't worked in 12 years."

King learned a great deal about directing from George Romero (left), who directed *Creepshow*. The two collaborated on other films based on King's novels, such as *Tales from the Darkside: The Movie* and *The Dark Half*.

of the city as organism." In the epic tradition, the characters descend into the underworld, the sewers of Derry.

A significant theme in King's works is one in which grown-ups must be able to communicate with the child within in order to tap into the imagination that is rooted in childhood. To survive, adults must be able to call up the ingenuity and simple faith that belong to their childhood. The critic Tony Magistrale finds King's romantic view of childhood positively Wordsworthian: it is the child who lights the way to moral excellence.

While his own children were young, King saw how strongly a child's imagination works. The Kings used to watch the world news at dinnertime, but one day Joe, who was then eight years old, turned pale, left the table, and started to vomit. The news was far too real to him. According to King, children have not yet learned to emotionally detach themselves from distant events the way adults do. The Kings cured Joe's stomach problems simply by watching the late news after their son had gone to bed.

Although the Kings do not have an ordinary lifestyle, Stephen says, "We want order in our lives," which is why Tabitha always packs clothes for her husband when he makes business trips. She knows which pants match which shirt, and so on. That need for order also explains why King wears his "rattiest" jacket to television interviews: it is his lucky jacket.

Fearful of jeopardizing other people's money and unwilling to leave Tabitha and the children, King had over the course of his career turned down several offers to direct movies based on his novels. But in an effort to gain more control over the content of those movies, King finally decided to try his hand at directing. *Maximum Overdrive,* the 13th film adapted from King's fiction, was based on an early short story and picks up on the monstrous-machine theme. In the movie, a passing comet causes machines to come to life and ultimately attack their makers.

The set, the Dixie Boy Truckstop, was constructed by the producer Dino De Laurentiis, whose film studio is located just outside Wilmington, North Carolina. In temperatures ranging from 90 to 110 degrees Fahrenheit, King worked from sunrise to sunset, then looked at rushes (also called dailies, the prints of scenes from the previous day, which are processed overnight), and when he finally fell into bed after his 18-hour day, he would dream about that day's work. An added complication was that his cinematographer, Armando Nannuzzi, did not speak any English, and the camera operator did not speak much either. The film credits list the interpreters.

King learned about directing by watching George A. Romero, who directed the touchstone modern horror movie *Night of the Living Dead* (1968) and King's own *Creepshow* (1982), at work and on the job. King had chosen to direct *Maximum Overdrive* because the machines seemed simpler to work with than people, whose moods and temperaments he feared would slow down production. Instead, he found machines quite inimical. Machines made trouble, stalling when the script called for speed or slipping into forward when they were asked to die.

For King, the actors were the happy surprise. Cooperative, talented, and hardworking, they gave their best and put up with incredibly unpleasant conditions. For example, one actress had to sit day after day in a load of rotting watermelons. Each time, she had to sit among maggots, but she did her job without complaining. King said actors "don't complain. They really want to work, and to please you. And . . . they're good!" King has a cameo in the picture—he tries to withdraw money from a bank automatic-teller machine and is insulted by it.

Though *Maximum Overdrive* was a flop at the box office, King found the entire moviemaking process fascinating. He figured that people who considered his work vulgar and tasteless ought nevertheless to recognize the "spirit behind it . . . a combination of [the English satiric comedians] Monty Python and [the mysterious Victorian murderer] Jack the Ripper."

However, the 1986 movie *Stand By Me,* directed by Rob Reiner for Columbia Pictures and based on King's 1977 semiautobiographical novella, "The Body," was a major critical success. Most people do not even realize that this coming-of-age tale is based on a

Kathy Bates, wielding a sledgehammer, portrays nurse Annie Wilkes in *Misery,* the 1990 movie based on King's novel. Bates won an Academy Award for Best Actress for her role as the crazed fan who holds a best-selling writer (played by James Caan) prisoner.

Stephen King short story. Richard Dreyfuss, who represents King, narrates the tale of boyhood friendship and exploits that occurred in the summer of 1959. King said, "It's all autobiographical in a sense, but writers all lie. You know, they make up the good parts."

Critics called the movie "irresistible." Set in the woods near Castle Rock, the story relates the adventures of four young boys who follow a railroad track searching for the body of a missing boy. King told Stephen Schaefer that the characters were based on his friends, all three of whom had died—one in a house fire, the others in car accidents. After viewing the movie, King told Reiner, "It was upsetting to sit there and see all these kids I grew up with on screen, brought back to life when—well, you can't ever get them back."

By July 11, 1986, King was an authentic celebrity, outshining his buddy, singer Bruce Springsteen, according to that day's edition of the *Maine Times*. When a girl

In 1987, Tabitha King receives an honorary doctorate from her alma mater, the University of Maine at Orono, as her husband, Stephen, proudly applauds. Stephen has strongly supported Tabitha with her writing efforts— she has published several novels on her own.

approached the two, she asked only for King's autograph. King even appeared in an American Express commercial, playing himself, disappearing into the mist. "When I'm not recognized, it just kills me," he says in the commercial.

In 1987, King published four books: *The Dark Tower II: The Drawing of the Three,* the Viking edition of *The Eyes of the Dragon, Misery,* and *The Tommyknockers.*

The Tommyknockers, begun in 1982, shares *The Talisman*'s, that is, Stephen King's, obsession with the dangers of nuclear weapons and the possibility of radiation pollution that could poison the earth for thousands of years. He concludes that the risks of developing certain technologies far outweigh the possible benefits.

Misery is the story of Paul Sheldon, an innocent, popular, and wealthy writer of pulp romance novels, as King is a best-selling writer of horror novels. Sheldon

In Cambridge, Massachusetts, King and author John Irving (left) read from their works in an effort to raise money for little-known short story writer Andre Dubus, who was severely injured in a car accident in July 1986.

would like to write more serious books, but he is kept prisoner and crippled by a powerful nurse, Annie Wilkes, a crazed fan who demands that Sheldon continue to write the trash for which he became famous. Twice within the novel King refers to John Fowles's first novel, *The Collector,* in which a collector, attracted and infuriated by a beautiful artist, kidnaps and torments her.

In 1988, his radio station, WZON, suffered from low ratings and money problems. King sold it but later bought it back. WZON, now owned by the Zone Corporation, a not-for-profit organization of which King is president, broadcasts local sports events. Later the same year, Tabitha published her third book, *Pearl.*

The movie version of *Misery,* released in 1990, was directed by Rob Reiner. Starring James Caan, it was another critical and box-office success. Kathy Bates, who plays Annie Wilkes, won an Academy Award in the Best Actress category.

In *Misery,* Paul Sheldon remembers a game called Can You? that he played as a child at the Malden Community Center day camp. The children would sit in a circle and the counselor would start telling a story and then pick a child to quickly continue it. If the chosen child took too long to begin the story or if his story did not seem to be a logical continuation, he had to leave the circle. The child's game reminded Sheldon of what Annie Wilkes was forcing him to do—hurriedly write a story that she would accept so he would be set free. *"The name of the game then was Can You?, Paulie, and that's the name of the game now, isn't it?"* novelist Sheldon thinks. *"Can you, Paul? Yeah. That's how I survive . . . if you want me to take you away, to scare you or involve you or make you cry or grin, yeah. I can. I can bring it to you and keep bringing it until you holler uncle. I am able. I CAN."* King now knew for certain *he* could play the game and had succeeded in doing just what he had set out to do.

8 ★ The Bogeyman Is Here To Stay

STEPHEN KING CREDITS CHIP McGRATH of the *New Yorker* with giving him "the opportunity of a lifetime" and coaxing "the best nonfiction writing of my life out of me."

"Head Down" appeared in the *New Yorker* in the spring of 1990. King followed his son Owen, who was 12 years old and a member of Bangor West, a hometown baseball team, to the Little League State Championship. Then King wrote a piece about the team's competition.

Though King had earned his first money as a writer when he was "the entire sports department" of the weekly *Lisbon Enterprise* while in high school, in the introduction to *Nightmares & Dreamscapes,* his collection of short stories that includes this nonfiction piece, King confesses that he found the undertaking of writing about the Bangor West All-Star Little League team daunting.

First, his son's team had to win the District 3 Championship, a feat Bangor West had last accomplished 18 years before. Not only did the team win the

---

Stephen King throws the first pitch at a Little League All-Star Championship game in Old Town, Maine, in August 1989. His son Owen was a member of the Bangor West baseball team, which won the Maine State Championship. King wrote an essay about the team and the competition that appeared in the *New Yorker,* and he used his earnings from the article to buy new uniforms for the Bangor teams.

district championship, but Bangor West, the only team to wear "shirts of many colors bearing the names of their team sponsors" rather than matching uniforms, went on to win the Maine State Championship as well.

King described their coaches, including Dave Mansfield, who was named Amateur Coach of the Year by the United States Baseball Federation, and members of the 1989 team of 12-year-olds, who ranged in size from five feet three inches all the way up to Owen, who stood six feet two inches tall and weighed 200 pounds. The club crossed class lines, welding farm kids, town kids, good students, and troublemakers into a championship team. A sociologist's study King had once read pointed out that Little League, though it passed on the values of fair play, hard work, and team spirit, did not usually change individuals. But coach Mansfield's assessment was that the team was what the season was all about. Boys of all backgrounds had become the championship team of 1989. Win or lose, they loved one another because they were a team. King used his wages from the *New Yorker* article to buy new uniforms for the Bangor Little League teams.

An avid Boston Red Sox fan, King shaves his bushy beard at the beginning of baseball season and sadly stows his electric razor away in a drawer after the last game of the World Series. "To me," King has said, "the beginning and the end of the baseball season mark, or symbolically bookend, summer," when it is too hot for a blanketlike beard. "In wintertime when it's cold it covers your face, and where I am, in Maine, it's really cold."

In his notes to *Nightmares & Dreamscapes,* King again tells readers that what writers do is hard work. The magic is "that instant when the story pops into a writer's head." A writer can reconstruct where he or she was when the idea arrived and even trace elements that "combined to give him his idea, but the *idea itself* is a new thing,

Tabitha (center) and Stephen King receive a key to the city in August 1992 for donating $1 million to build a baseball park in Bangor. The ballpark is intended for baseball players of all ages and includes seating for 1,500 people, concession stands, and lighting for night games.

something created from nothing. He paraphrases the poet Marianne Moore and calls it "a real toad in an imaginary garden."

King's latest collection of short stories includes "Dolan's Cadillac." He credits his brilliant brother, David, who finished college at 18, with doing the research for the story, a chore Stephen avoids whenever possible. David King produced a videotape, complete with sand and model cars. He included instructions for hot-wiring highway department bulldozers capable of burying a Cadillac that were so precise that King had to change details to be sure no real-life thief found the perfect recipe for thievery in his story.

In "Umney's Last Case," King pays homage to Raymond Chandler and Ross Macdonald by patterning his milieu and writing style on theirs. And he ends his notes on "Brooklyn August," his salute to Brooklyn's Ebbets Field, with wise words: "Read a few good books, and if one of your brothers or sisters falls down and you

King poses on the set of *Stephen King's Graveyard Shift,* a 1990 movie based on the short story that is in the *Night Shift* collection. King wrote most of the story in the *Maine Campus* office while he attended college.

see it happen, pick him or her up. After all, next time *you* might be the one who needs a hand."

And, in a final parable, "The Beggar and the Diamond," King tells critics who disparage him because of his popularity that he gives readers stories that they can absorb and make good use of in their lives.

In 1989, King published *The Dark Half,* and in 1991, he published *Needful Things,* two-thirds of a trilogy that also includes "The Sun Dog," a novella included in the collection *Four Past Midnight.* Actually, King tried unsuccessfully to get Viking to publish *The Dark Half* as a collaboration between King and his pen name Richard Bachman, who King says perished of "cancer of the pseudonym" in 1985. King wanted to resurrect Bachman to make apparent the parallels between himself and the author-protagonist of *The Dark Half.* In a Waldenbooks interview, King said that Bachman is his darker, more violent side, just as George Stark is the suppressed evil twin of the protagonist, Thad Beaumont. And the *New York Times* critic Christopher Lehmann-Haupt's review describes *The Dark Half* as "a writer's demon."

King notes that his subject matter is changing. Now that his own children are older, there are few children in his current work, despite his fascination with his own childhood.

Needful Things is an exception. "I was fascinated as an adult with the period when my own children were growing up. And I'm interested in the mythic power that childhood holds over our imagination and, in particular, the point at which the adult is able to link up with his or her own childhood past and the powers therein," King told Tony Magistrale.

Needful Things also documents the end of the fictional town of Castle Rock, Maine, the beloved hometown of many King characters. But King felt as if he had done everything he could do in that particular world. He was finished with those characters and wanted to start anew.

In 1992, King published *Gerald's Game* and *Dolores Claiborne,* in which he employs in both novels the 1963 assassination of President John F. Kennedy and the last total solar eclipse visible in northern New England until the year 2016. These two books, their plots connected tangentially, are the beginning of another fictional world—also located in Maine.

Set on a tiny Maine island, *Dolores Claiborne* is dedicated to King's mother, Ruth, and features an extremely strong heroine. As early as *Carrie,* King had tried to create female characters who were more than "bitches or zeroes," which is the normal way of portraying women in American fiction, according to Leslie Fiedler's provocative study, *Love and Death in the American Novel.* "Not only is the protagonist a woman, she's also an older woman who is *the* major character." Other characters "are always in her shadow; she dominates this particular landscape." King told Tony Magistrale, "I did a good job. Readers are going to be pleased with the woman they find there." And, indeed, they were.

The year 1993 brought movies of *The Dark Half* and *Needful Things,* both now available in video stores, as are just about all of King's movies. A four-hour version of *The Tommyknockers* was televised in May 1993 on ABC. In his review, John Leonard said it "might be preposterous, but I enjoyed every throbbing minute of it."

King continues to deal with the problems that are the price of fame. In April 1991, a crazed fan broke into the

Kings' home, claiming he had a bomb and terrorizing Tabitha. The same year, a woman in New Jersey sued King, claiming that he had broken into her home and stolen her story ideas. The case went to court, and the woman lost. With good reason, King has grown wary of attending book conventions.

King performs at charity benefits with a music group of authors and journalists called the Rockbottom Remainders. An anthology of their work, *Midlife Confidential,* was published in the fall of 1994. The group has toured for Literacy for America.

In 1994, the Rockbottom Remainders added go-go dancers, among them humorist and syndicated columnist Cynthia Heimel, author of *Get Your Tongue Out of My Mouth, I'm Kissing You Goodbye.* Heimel's *Village Voice* column of June 14, 1994, described both that year's American Booksellers Association Convention in Los Angeles, California, and the unexpected pleasures of performing in a gilt cage.

King (right) sings and plays guitar with musician Al Kooper in Anaheim, California, where the American Booksellers Association Convention was held in 1992. King is a member of the Rockbottom Remainders, a music group composed of authors, journalists, and cartoonists, all of whom have dreamed of playing rock and roll in the spotlight.

Other members of the group include authors Amy Tan, K. Friedman, and Ken Follett; humorists Dave Barry and Roy Blount, Jr.; cartoonist Kathi Goldmark; and Matt Groening, the creator of "The Simpsons." Writer Erica Jong dropped by, and Bruce Springsteen stopped in to sing "Gloria."

As the television event of 1994, "The Stand,"the King tale of a plague that wipes out most of the population, captured a huge viewing audience for the better part of a week. More than 33 million people watched the first of the four-night, eight-hour miniseries that aired in May, and each night earned generally favorable reviews. Mick Garris, an author of horror stories, directed the screenplay that was written by King.

One of the most powerful scenes turned out to be one of King's favorites from all the way back in 1979, when he described it to an interviewer for *Yankee* magazine.

Stephen and Tabitha King receive the Norbert X. Dowd Award for community service at the annual Greater Bangor Chamber of Commerce dinner in 1992. The Kings have made monetary contributions to the Old Town Library and the baseball park, among other donations that have been kept secret. "We're glad to be a part of Bangor," King said at the dinner. "Whatever we've done for Bangor was the result of what Bangor had done for us."

In 1993, Stephen King and suspense writer John Grisham arrive at the National Book Awards ceremony in New York. Upon entering the Plaza Hotel, where the affair was held, Grisham asked King, "Do you ever scare yourself?" to which King replied, "Yes."

Trying to escape from New York City, the protagonist Larry Underwood walks through the Lincoln Tunnel, which is jammed with hundreds of cars filled with the bodies of flu victims who died before they could get out of the city. He begins to think he hears footsteps and car doors opening and slamming shut. He is terrified, and so is the viewer.

Millions of King readers welcomed a new novel, *Insomnia,* in September 1994. In October, riding along back roads on his Harley Davidson motorcycle, King completed a 10-city promotional tour of independent bookstores to help publicize *Insomnia* in the smaller establishments, which he prefers to the commercialism of the large chain bookstores. At each stop, King presigned copies of his novel and then went to a nearby auditorium to give a speech about the importance of independent bookselling. He attended the 1994 meeting of the American Booksellers Association in Los Angeles, where he promoted *Insomnia* with T-shirt and poster tie-ins.

Stephen King has earned millions of dollars. The University of Maine at Orono now has a collection of King manuscripts and memorabilia. Clearly, he never has to write another word for financial gain. But in the 1983 *Playboy* interview, King said, "Writing is necessary for my sanity. As a writer, I can externalize my fears and insecurities and night terrors on paper, which is what people pay shrinks a small fortune to do. They pay me for psychoanalyzing myself in print. And in the process, I'm able to 'write myself sane,' as that fine poet Anne Sexton put it. It's an old technique of therapists, you know: get the patient to write out his demons."

For King, as his many writer personae testify, "the written word [is] a means for regaining control over [the writers'] own lives and the lives of those who touch them." In his fiction, the process of writing always has a stabilizing affect on the writer, with the exception of the monumentally blocked Jack Torrance of *The Shining*.

According to Magistrale, "King's writer-protagonists make their lives their craft, but they also owe their lives to their craft." He said, "The art—the skill of writing—is real magic, and the individual . . . who utilizes it must also stand in awe of it."

For King, writers are neither mad nor sick, as the romantics maintain. Instead, art is how artists attain "sanity and salvation: the dark chaos of the world can be managed, but only through the illumination of a mind that has labored to gain control over itself."

King tells his readers in *Danse Macabre* that "fiction is the truth inside the lie, and in the tale of horror, as in any other tale, the same rule applies as much now as when Aristophanes [the Greek playwright of the 4th century B.C.] told his horror tale of the frogs: morality is telling the truth as your heart knows it [from Aristophanes' play, *Frogs,* in which Aeschylus and Euripides discuss their own works and criticize and parody each other's]."

In King's view, lies distort and oppress. The writer's business of

King pets Clovis, the hero of *Stephen King's Sleepwalkers,* a movie for which he wrote the original screenplay. King had high hopes for the film, which is about ancient catlike creatures who feed on the life force of innocent teenage girls, but critics called the movie a disaster.

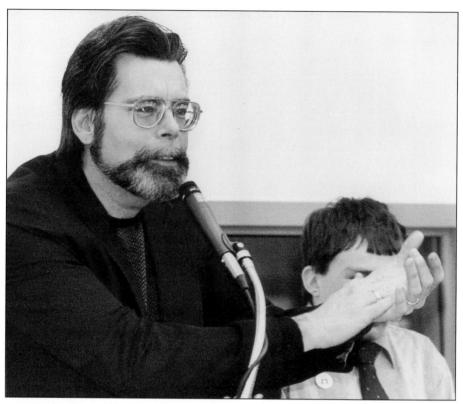

King speaks at the Eastern Maine Medical Center pediatric wing dedication ceremony in January 1994. He was the honorary chairman of the fund-raising effort to which he donated a substantial amount of money. The cochairman of the committee said, "To have a man of his stature join the campaigning team is obviously going to have a positive influence on our fund-raising efforts."

telling the truth results from disciplined "work and honest self-examination." As Magistrale states, not only does King stare into the abyss, he writes about it.

He no longer drinks and rarely smokes, but he coaches Little League and supports the writers he respects. And King continues to write for at least two or three hours each day, seven days a week, in the big Victorian house with the bats and spiders on the wrought-iron fence.

Some years ago, he selected his epitaph, one he had originally imagined carved over the fireplace of the massive brownstone he described in his novella "The Breathing Method": "IT IS THE TALE, NOT HE WHO TELLS IT." He says, "Just that and no name."

NOVELS

Carrie. 1974. Reprint. New York: New American Library, 1975.

Christine. 1983. Reprint. New York: New American Library, 1984.

Cujo. 1981. Reprint: New York: New American Library, 1982.

Cycle of the Werewolf. 1983, Reprint. New York: New American Library, 1984.

The Dark Half. 1989. Reprint. New York: New American Library, 1990.

The Dark Tower: The Gunslinger. 1984. Reprint. New York: New American Library, 1988.

The Dark Tower II: The Drawing of the Three. New York: New American Library, 1987.

The Dark Tower III: The Wastelands. New York: New American Library, 1991.

The Dark Tower IV: Wizard and Glass. New Hampshire: Donald M. Grant, 1997.

The Dead Zone. 1979. Reprint. New York: New American Library, 1980.

Desperation. New York: Viking, 1996

Dolores Claiborne. 1992. Reprint. New York: New American Library, 1994.

The Eyes of the Dragon. 1987. Reprint. New York: New American Library, 1987.

Firestarter. 1980. Reprint. New York: New American Library, 1981.

Gerald's Game. 1992. Reprint. New York: New American Library/Dutton, 1993.

The Green Mile Part One: The Two Dead Girls. New York: New American Library, 1996.

The Green Mile Part Two: The Mouse on the Mile. New York: New American Library, 1996.

The Green Mile Part Three: Coffey's Hands. New York: New American Library, 1996.

The Green Mile Part Four: The Bad Death of Eduard Delacroix. New York: New American Library, 1996.

The Green Mile Part Five: Night Journey. New York: New American Library, 1996.

The Green Mile Part Six: Coffey on the Mile. New York: New American Library, 1996.

Insomnia. New York: Viking, 1994.

It. 1986. Reprint. New York: New American Library, 1987.

[Richard Bachman, pseud.] *The Long Walk.* New York: New American Library, 1979.

Misery. 1987. Reprint. New York: New American Library, 1987.

Needful Things. 1991. Reprint. New York: New American Library/Dutton, 1992.

Pet Semetary. 1983. Reprint. New York: New American Library, 1984.

[Richard Bachman, pseud.] *Rage*. New York: New American Library, 1977.

[Richard Bachman, pseud.] *The Regulators*. New York: E.P. Dutton, 1996.

[Richard Bachman, pseud.] *Roadworks*. New York: New American Library, 1981.

Rose Madder. New York: Viking, 1995.

[Richard Bachman, pseud.] *The Running Man*. New York: New American Library, 1982.

'Salem's Lot. 1975. Reprint. New York: New American Library, 1978.

The Shining. 1977. Reprint. New York: New American Library, 1978.

The Stand. 1978. 2d ed., rev. and unexpurg. New York: New American Library/Dutton, 1990

(with Peter Straub.) *The Talisman*. 1984. Reprint. New York: Berkeley, 1985.

[Richard Bachman, pseud.] *Thinner*. New York: New American Library, 1984.

The Tommyknockers. 1987. Reprint. New York: New American Library, 1988.

COLLECTIONS

The Bachman Books: Four Early Novels by Stephen King. 1985. Reprint. New York: New American Library, 1986.

Creepshow. New York: New American Library, 1982.

Different Seasons. 1982. Reprint. New York: New American Library, 1983.

Four Past Midnight. 1990. Reprint. New York: New American Library/Dutton, 1991.

Nightmares & Dreamscapes. 1993. Reprint. New York: New American Library/ Dutton, 1994.

Night Shift. 1978. Reprint. New York: New American Library, 1979.

Skeleton Crew. 1985. Reprint. New York: New American Library, 1986.

NON–FICTION

Danse Macabre. 1981. Reprint. New York: Berkeley, 1982.

Nightmares in the Sky: Gargoyles and Grotesques. New York: Viking, 1988.

Further Reading ★ ★ ★ ★ ★ ★ ★ ★ ★ ★ ★ ★ ★ ★ ★ ★

Beahm, George, ed. *The Stephen King Companion.* Kansas City, MO: Andrews and McMeel, 1989.

Magistrale, Tony. *Landscapes of Fear: Stephen King's American Gothic.* Bowling Green, OH: Bowling Green State University Popular Press, 1988.

————. *Stephen King: The Second Decade, "Danse Macabre" to "The Dark Half."* New York: Twayne, 1992.

Reino, Joseph. *Stephen King: The First Decade, From "Carrie" to "Pet Sematary."* Boston: Twayne, 1988.

Spignesi, Stephen J. *The Complete Stephen King Encyclopedia: The Definitive Guide to the Works of America's Master of Horror.* Chicago: Contemporary Books, 1991.

Underwood, Tim, and Chuck Miller, eds. *Bare Bones: Conversations on Terror with Stephen King.* New York: McGraw-Hill, 1988.

————. *Feast of Fear: Conversations with Stephen King.* New York: Carroll & Graf, 1992.

Winter, Douglas E., ed. *The Art of Darkness: Life and Fiction of the Master of Macabre Stephen King.* New York: New American Library, 1986.

————"Stephen King." In *The Faces of Fear: Encounters with the Creators of Modern Horror.* New York: Berkley, 1985.

Chronology ★ ★ ★ ★ ★ ★ ★ ★ ★ ★ ★ ★ ★ ★ ★ ★

1947 Born Stephen Edwin King on September 21, in Portland, Maine

1962–66 Attends Lisbon Falls High School; begins writing *Getting It On*, later published as *Rage*.

1966–70 Attends University of Maine at Orono; writes a column "King's Garbage Truck," for the college paper; sells a short story, "The Glass Floor"; begins dating fellow student Tabitha Jane Spruce

1971 Marries Tabitha shortly after graduation; begins teaching English at Hampden Academy; daughter, Naomi, is born

1972–73 Son Joe is born; *Carrie* is accepted for publication by Doubleday

1974 *Carrie* is published; moves the family to Boulder, Colorado, where he writes *The Shining*; begins to develop *The Stand*

1975 *'Salem's Lot* is published; returns to Maine and buys a house in Bridgton; a depository for Stephen King material is established by the University of Maine at Orono

1976 Film version of *Carrie*, directed by Brian DePalma, is released.

1977 Son Owen is born; *The Shining* is published; using the pseudonym Richard Bachman for the first time, *Rage* is published.

1978 The first collection of short stories *Night Shift*, is published; becomes a writer-in-residence at the University of Maine at Orono; signs major book contract with New American Library

1980 Buys a Victorian mansion in Bangor; named *People* magazine's Writer of the Year; film version of *The Shining*, directed by Stanley Kubrick, is released

1981 His first work of nonfiction, *Danse Macabre*, is published

1982 Receives World Fantasy Award for "Do the Dead Sing?" (also known as "The Reach"), the British Fantasy Award for *Cujo*, and the Hugo Award for *Danse Macabre*; writes

script and acts in movie version of *Creepshow*

1983 Film versions of *Cujo*, *The Dead Zone*, and *Christine* are released

1984 Co-authors *The Talisman* with Peter Straub; *The Eyes of the Dragon* is published in limited edition; film versions of *Children of the Corn* and *Firestarter* are released

1985 Reveals Richard Bachman pseudonym; collection of first four Bachman books is published; *Cat's Eye*, a movie based on King's short stories, is released; *Silver Bullet*, a movie based on the novelette *Cycle of the Werewolf*, is released

1986 Directs *Maximum Overdrive*, a movie adapted from his short story "Trucks"; *Stand By Me* (the movie version of "The Body"), directed by Rob Reiner, is released

1987 *The Running Man* (a Bachman book) and *Creepshow II* are released

1989 *The Dark Half* is published in the largest first-edition printing in history; movie version of *Pet Semetary* is released

1990 The complete edition of *The Stand* is published; movie versions of "Graveyard Shift," *It*, and *Misery*, are released

1993 *Nightmares & Dreamscapes*, a collection of short stories, is published; film version of *Needful Things* is released

1994 Televised version of *The Stand* is broadcast; embarks on first book tour in almost a decade to promote *Insomnia*

1995 Movie version of *Dolores Claiborne* is released; *Rose Madder* is published; *The Shawshank Redemption*, a story from "Different Seasons," is released on film to critical acclaim and a Best Picture nomination

1996 *The Regulators* (the last Bachman novel) and *Desperation* are published; begins *The Green Mile* series

1997 The six books of *The Green Mile* series are available; becomes first author to have six books simultaneously on *The New York Times, USA Today*, and *Publishers Weekly* best-seller lists; *The Dark Tower IV: Wizard and Glass* is released

Index ★★★★★★★★★★★★★★★★★★★★★★★★

Amy Keyishian is a graduate of Barnard College. She is a freelance writer who has also worked in film, computer games, stand-up comedy, and publishing.

Marjorie Keyishian, Amy's mother, is a Brooklyn-born teacher at Fairleigh Dickinson University and a freelance journalist, as well as a published writer of fiction and poetry.

Leeza Gibbons is a reporter for and cohost of the nationally syndicated television program "Entertainment Tonight" and NBC's daily talk show "Leeza." A graduate of the University of South Carolina's School of Journalism, Gibbons joined the on-air staff of "Entertainment Tonight" in 1984 after cohosting WCBS-TV's "Two on the Town" in New York City. Prior to that, she cohosted "PM Magazine" on WFAA-TV in Dallas, Texas, and on KFDM-TV in Beaumont, Texas. Gibbons also hosts the annual "Miss Universe," "Miss U.S.A.," and "Miss Teen U.S.A." pageants, as well as the annual Hollywood Christmas Parade. She is active in a number of charities and has served as the national chairperson for the Spinal Muscular Atrophy Division of the Muscular Dystrophy Association; each September, Gibbons cohosts the National MDA Telethon with Jerry Lewis.